PETITION PROCEDURE
IN THE
COURT OF SESSION

PETITION PROCEDURE
IN THE
COURT OF SESSION

BY

WILLIAM W. McBRYDE, LL.B.(Edin.), Ph.D.(Glas.),
Solicitor,
Professor of Scots Law in the University of Dundee

AND

NORMAN J. DOWIE,
Clerk to the First Division of the Court of Session

SECOND EDITION

EDINBURGH
W. GREEN & SON LTD.
ST. GILES STREET
1988

First published in 1980

Second edition 1988

ISBN 0 414 00831 6

PRINTED IN GREAT BRITAIN BY
EASTERN PRESS

ADDENDUM

AFTER the text of this book had been passed for press, amendments to the Insolvency (Scotland) Rules 1986 appeared. On January 11, 1988 there will come into force the Insolvency (Scotland) Amendment Rules 1987 (S.I. 1987 No. 1921). These rules will apply to all insolvency proceedings which are governed by the Insolvency (Scotland) Rules 1986 whether or not the proceedings commenced before or after January 11, 1988. The new rules make 60 amendments to the 1986 rules and introduce five new forms. Of particular importance to court proceedings are: (1) a specific provision that a provisional liquidator need not produce evidence of caution provided it is averred that he is a qualified insolvency practitioner and he consents to act. This confirms present practice; (2) a time limit for the holding of meetings of creditors and contributories for the purpose of choosing a person to be liquidator of the company in place of the interim liquidator. The meeting must be held not later than 42 days after the date of the winding up order or such longer period as the court may allow. This cures a defect in section 138(3) of the Insolvency Act 1986 under which the interim liquidator was bound to call the meeting within a 28-day period but the section failed to specify when the meeting had to be held; (3) new provisions for the disposal of the sederunt book and the company's books and records by the responsible insolvency practitioner in any insolvency proceedings to which the rules apply. The new forms include (1) a notice to a court of the resignation of an administrator; (2) a statutory demand for payment of a debt within 21 days; (3) a statement of a claim by a creditor; and (4) a notice to the Registrar of Companies of the appointment of a liquidator. Old forms may be used until March 1, 1988.

FOREWORD

THIS, the second edition of the work of Professor McBryde and Mr. Dowie is, in my opinion, even better than its predecessor. It is written for practitioners by experts, and as a practical handbook upon a subject which is technical and unexciting, it has achieved to a remarkable degree, readability, accuracy and clarity. The first edition was a much needed practical guide for court practitioners, and in this second edition the authors have taken account of all the major changes, statutory and otherwise, which have taken place since 1980 to affect Petition practice. I do not rehearse them here, for they are identified in the Preface, and I would simply add that one of the virtues of this new edition is that it has not merely updated the procedural content of the work but has explained how in practice problems caused by certain deficiencies in our rules and in statutory provisions are being overcome. The Rules Review Group is, I am glad to say, well aware of these deficiencies and will, no doubt, in carrying out their task, attempt to remove them.

Emslie
Lord President   December 1987

PREFACE TO FIRST EDITION

THIS book gives a summary of the procedure followed in the Court of Session in the commoner petitions and, occasionally, where space allowed, in some petitions which are not so common. We have based our selection of items on our different experiences of the work of the petition department. To have included every possible item would have more than doubled the size of the book for little benefit to, and some financial burden for, many of its users. We hope to have provided a guide for most situations, and our purpose will have been fulfilled if we thereby leave more time for practitioners and court staff to consider the esoteric.

We have described the practice of the court, concentrating on what happens across the counter in the petition department, day in, day out. Anyone familiar with this work knows that there is some flexibility in practice, not all of it desirable. We have not hesitated to indicate a view of what the best practice is. Nor have we always restrained ourselves from being critical. This is not only with a hope for reform, but rather to indicate to the novice that if he finds some aspects of procedure puzzling, he is not alone.

It is customary in a preface to give thanks to all who have helped in the preparation of the book. We gladly do so, but trust they will not be offended by a general expression of our appreciation. Many have given us time and advice, from the most senior court staff to the porters whose help was given, perhaps unknowingly, when they unearthed for us hundreds of processes from the depths of Parliament House. To them all we are grateful. We wish, however, to thank in particular W. L. O'Connor, Accountant of Court, for his assistance. O. J. Brown, Principal Clerk of Session and Justiciary, gave permission and encouragement without which this book would not have been written. We hope that it justifies his faith.

We have tried to state the practice of the court at December 31, 1979.

W.McB.
N.D.   May 1980

PREFACE TO SECOND EDITION

SINCE the first edition of this book there have been major changes in both legislation and the practices of the court. The Bankruptcy (Scotland) Act 1985 was the most radical change in sequestration procedure for over a century. The Insolvency Act 1986 and its related subordinate legislation transformed liquidation procedure and introduced the concept of administration orders. All the new insolvency legislation continues to pose problems for court staff and practitioners. Some of the difficulties are caused by lack of familiarity with complex rules but in other cases doubts arise about how the new rules should be applied. There is now a more international aspect to petition procedure as legislation gives effect to international conventions. The need for recognition of the orders of other countries produced the Child Abduction and Custody Act 1985 and parts of both the Civil Jurisdiction and Judgments Act 1982 and the Family Law Act 1986. Edictal service has changed with a desire to bring our practice into line with that in EEC countries. The continuing programme of reform of family law has had an impact. Petition procedures have been introduced to deal with the Matrimonial Homes (Family Protection) (Scotland) Act 1981 and the Law Reform (Parent and Child) (Scotland) Act 1986. The introduction of judicial review by an Act of Sederunt has been popular and shows some of the best features of petition procedure which has been traditionally a summary procedure able to deal with complex and important issues.

Within the court there have been many administrative changes designed to improve the efficiency of the court. Inhibition is the only procedure by bill which most practitioners now come across and there is a long history of its use in the bill chamber which was the predecessor to the petition department. But inhibitions were being sought in such numbers that the application for an inhibition had to be taken out of the petition department. The petition department, however, continues to receive the many petitions for recall or restriction of inhibitions. The new practice on motions was designed to make more efficient use of judicial time and the practice affects every Outer House petition. The increasing use of *interim* orders shows the court working at speed and there has now been a concentration on the true function of a caveat which has raised problems that have yet to be resolved.

As the text of this book was reaching its final form an Act of Sederunt appeared which made significant changes to petition procedure. The Inner House ceased to have jurisdiction at first instance to deal with some trust petitions and many applications under the Companies Acts. The Act of Sederunt affected the averments on jurisdiction to be made in a petition and the form of a motion to grant the prayer of an unopposed petition.

This book is a much expanded and revised version of the first edition. It would be impossible to deal with every possible petition in a book whose aims and size are both modest. Petitions or other applications under the Companies Act 1985 could themselves form the subject of a book. Nor can we, in the space available, consider all the problems of the substantive law. But we think that in the context of the overall work of the petition department there are very few petitions which are anything like common and which do not have a mention and we tend to restrict our comments to problems which experience has shown arise in practice. Petition procedure is, within limits, a very flexible procedure and it should be possible to adapt the procedures mentioned here to any form of petition.

Our previous edition was, to a large extent, a description of settled practices of the court. The multitude of recent changes has meant that often in this edition we have had to speculate on what the practice should be. This has increased the chances that we will be either wrong or unhelpful. We apologise, but we hope that the profession will appreciate some guidance on both the known and the unknown, even if this poses a hazard for the reputation of the authors.

It would be impossible to write a book like this without the help of many people. The staff in the Court of Session have patiently and efficiently answered our queries. We thank everyone who has given us time and assistance and, in particular, A. McClure Campbell, the Principal Clerk of Session and Justiciary, William McCulloch, Depute Clerk of Session and Justiciary, David Shand, Assistant Clerk of Session, and Robert Cockburn, Assistant Clerk of Session. Valuable assistance was provided by Derek Addison, Depute Accountant of Court.

Drafts of some chapters were commented on by Professor M. C. Meston and Paul Beaumont, both of Aberdeen University.

We have tried to state the practice of the court at September 1, 1987. In writing the book it was assumed that the Family Law Act 1986 was fully in force.

W.McB.
N.D.   November 1987

CONTENTS

TABLE OF CASES

TABLE OF STATUTES

TABLE OF INSOLVENCY (SCOTLAND) RULES 1986

TABLE OF RULES OF COURT

CHAPTER 1

INTRODUCTION

The petition department

One of the remarkable features of the Court of Session is the existence of two procedures to initiate cases. The summons is linked to the work of the general department; the petition is presented in the petition department. It is not necessary for present purposes to explain how this division arose and its consequences or to examine the fascinating history of the development of the court, much of which has not been fully researched. But the division into two systems of procedure affects the working lives of those involved in the court and some explanation, brief and incomplete as it is, may be of interest.

The petition department was created by the Administration of Justice (Scotland) Act 1933, s. 24 (2). To a large extent its predecessor was the bill chamber. Although some petitions were not presented to the bill chamber it was the procedure of the chamber which influenced petition practice. The bill chamber had its origins in the early years of the Court of Session. When John Spotiswood was teaching law students in his "College of the Law of Scotland" around the time of the Union of 1707, he explained that there was a summary procedure upon a bill which was not tied to the formalities of an ordinary process. Two matters commonly dealt with by bills were suspensions and advocations. Both these could be matters of urgency. To suspend the operation of a decree, particularly when imprisonment was a normal remedy, was not a matter to consider at leisure. Advocation involved the challenge of an interlocutor of an inferior court and effective intervention required speed. To this day suspension and interdict is a petition department concern with a unique procedure which reflects the bill chamber as the place for the interim remedy and the separate jurisdiction of the Court of Session as the forum for detailed consideration of matters such as perpetual interdict. The petition department retains an anomalous administrative role in sheriff court appeals. The introduction of judicial review in 1985 has revived the role of the department in the exercise of the supervisory jurisdiction of the court over inferior tribunals. The procedure by bill has all but disappeared. It is found in the process of inhibition, but the great increase in the use of inhibitions had the effect that for administrative reasons bills for letters of

1

inhibition ceased to be presented in the petition department in 1986 (see Chapter 12).

The summary nature of petition procedure does lead to the suggestion that complex matters are inappropriate for a petition. For example, the court may be petitioned to order an arbiter to proceed but in a situation of any complexity a petition might not be the correct procedure (*Watson* v. *Robertson* (1895) 22 R. 362). The informality of the procedure in a petition by trustees for directions might lead to petition procedure being inappropriate in some cases (see p. 157). In a petition under the Forfeiture Act 1982 it was observed that a declarator might be more suitable if testamentary provisions required to be considered (*Paterson, Petr.*, 1986 S.L.T. 121). The appointment of a judicial factor might not be made if disputed and difficult questions were in issue (*Heggie* v. *Davidson*, 1973 S.L.T. (Notes) 47). Nevertheless judicial review procedure shows how complex matters may be dealt with successfully in a summary manner.

At times petition procedure can be very speedy. An example is the ease with which property and documents may be recovered under section 1 of the Administration of Justice (Scotland) Act 1972 (see Chapter 7). But the procedure should not be simplified too much. There were judicial strictures from Lord Cameron when parties presented a petition and answers which had been adjusted and asked for a decision without any order for intimation, service or answers (*Macallan-Glenlivet plc* v. *Speymalt Whisky Distributors Ltd.*, 1983 S.L.T. 348). Nevertheless the petition was heard with a joint minute being lodged to deal with the failures to follow the rules.

To the petition department belongs all procedure initiated by way of petition. A Royal Commission on the court explained in 1927 the difference between a summons and a petition in this way:

"The object of a summons is to enforce a pursuer's legal right against a defender who resists it, or to protect a legal right which the defender is infringing; the object of a petition, on the other hand, is to obtain from the administrative jurisdiction of the court power to do something or to require something to be done, which is just and proper should be done, but which the petitioner has no legal right to do or to require, apart from judicial authority. The contentious character of the proceedings which follow a summons necessitates a higher degree of formality than is appropriate to an *ex parte* application such as a petition, even though opposed; hence the distinction between the 'solemn' procedure in an action and the 'summary' procedure in a petition."

In *Tomkins* v. *Cohen*, 1951 S.C. 22 at p. 23, Lord Keith observed:

> "A petition is an *ex parte* application addressed to the Lords of Council and Session and seeks their aid for some purpose or other, *e.g.*, by supplying some deficiency of power in the petitioner, in protecting pupils and minors, by exercising some statutory jurisdiction, or the *nobile officium*, in a variety of matters. We are entirely masters of procedure in a petition, subject to any regulations thereanent made by Act of Sederunt . . ."

So it is that a petition does not proceed, like a summons, in the name of the sovereign requiring the defender to do something. A petition is addressed to the Lords of Council and Session. It may be served on many people, but it is unusual for answers to be lodged except in cases of suspension and interdict, judicial review, and petitions which relate to children. It is uncommon for proceedings to go as far as a record and a proof on a contested petition is unusual. Many petitions involve the appointment of an individual to an office or applications incidental to that office. The petition requests action by the court rather than action by a defender.

The records of the petition department

Within the petition department several records are kept. Amongst these is the petition register which is, at present, divided into 18 categories and each petition, note or other application is entered under the appropriate heading. This produces a reference number. For example the reference P6/2/1988 would mean that this was the sixth curatory or factory petition presented in 1988, curatory and factory cases being the second division of the register. Caveats are maintained with an index. A fee book records the fees incurred by solicitors who are billed by the cashier. A minute book is kept. Transmission books record the transfer of processes to other court offices.

It may assist those who have to work with the department to know how processes are filed. Processes are put into bolls which are arranged alphabetically according to subject matter. For example, a petition for the appointment of a trustee would be filed with other processes in the appropriate boll under the name of the trust or truster, *i.e.* under the name of the estate which is the subject of the petition (a similar rule applies to curatory, factory and liquidation processes). If a solicitor is trying to trace the process and all that he knows is that the petitioner was a Mr. A, there are going to be problems. The process will not be filed under the name of the petitioner. If the year of presentation of the petition is known the appropriate petition register may be of assistance, although entries in it will be chronological and not alphabetical. If the process is no longer active it may have been transferred to the records department in the basement of the Court of Session. The process can be traced provided that its reference number is known. The Extractor has a record of processes which have been extracted and the petition department have records of other processes which are no longer in their possession. After five years, except in unfinished curatory, factory and liquidation cases, processes are transmitted for storage to the Scottish Record Office (rule 32A). It is possible to arrange for a process in the Record Office to be retransmitted to the Court of Session and a fee is now charged by the Record Office for this service. Reasons for wishing to examine a process which appears to be inactive include the need to obtain a certified copy interlocutor, the approval of accounts of expenses, and the use of the case as a precedent.

Form of process

The form and size of the papers which make up a process are stated in rule 19. The form of petition is regulated by rule 191. Each step of process must be lodged bearing the same reference number as the petition (rule 194).

Inner House petitions must be marked "Inner House" on the backing (rule 190). When a petition is presented in the Inner House 10 copies of the petition must be lodged. This rule applies also to the reports of reporters and other principal documents listed in rule 26. The reason for requiring 10 copies is that one is required for the process, four for the judges, three for the three law libraries, and two for the reporters (1954 S.L.T. (News) 218). Whether the expense of this is justified in the case of the large number of unopposed petitions is a moot point. Only four copies of productions are lodged with any Inner House petition.

In Outer House petitions a copy is lodged in the box for the Advocates' Library. A copy of the petition, and other principal writs, is lodged in the box for the Accountant of Court in sequestrations, curatories, judicial factories, and applications for superintendence orders under section 17 or the Trusts (Scotland) Act 1921. These practices do not always produce consistent results. For example, the Accountant will receive a copy of a petition for sequestration but not of a petition to the *nobile officium* in a sequestration because the latter is an Inner House petition.

A process consists of an inventory of process, a petition, an interlocutor sheet, a duplicate inventory of process, a certified copy of the petition, a motion sheet and a minute of proceedings (rule 20). A small saving in expense which is not well known is that rule 20 provides that no minute of proceedings need be lodged in a petition unless and until answers are lodged. It must be admitted, however, that the rule is unsatisfactory because the minute of proceedings may be used in uncontested petitions. Entries may be made in it in trust variation petitions, *cy-près* applications and in undefended proofs which may occur in petitions for the custody of children. The minute of proceedings is almost invariably used in petitions for judicial review.

A solicitor is not entitled to borrow a process unless he has a place of business in Edinburgh (Solicitors (Scotland) Act 1980, s. 29 (1)).

Form of petition

The form of petition is regulated by rule 191 and by any rules specifically applicable to the type of petition in question.

The Act of Sederunt (Rules of Court Amendment No. 4) (Miscellaneous) 1987 (S.I. 1987 No. 1206) made a material change to the form of a petition by the addition of a new rule 191 (*aa*) which states:

> "The narrative of the petition shall include a paragraph stating—
> (i) the ground of jurisdiction of the court, unless jurisdiction would arise only if the respondent prorogated the jurisdiction of the court (without contesting jurisdiction);
> (ii) where appropriate, whether there is reason to believe that there exists an agreement prorogating the jurisdiction of a court in a particular country; and
> (iii) whether proceedings involving the same cause or matter are in subsistence between the parties in a country to which the Convention in Schedule 1 to the Civil Jurisdiction and Judgments Act 1982 applies, unless the court has exclusive jurisdiction."

One difficulty which arises is that the ground of jurisdiction in respect of several types of petition is far from clear. At appropriate places in the text we mention matters relating to jurisdiction but we cannot provide a comprehensive treatment of jurisdiction in the space available to us (although such a treatment is much needed).

Counsel who drafts a petition would assist considerably his or her instructing solicitor if the requirements of the new rule 197 (*e*) were anticipated. This requires a motion to grant the prayer of an unopposed petition to state both the jurisdiction of the court and the domicile of the respondent. This difficult requirement is considered later (p. 13). If the petition avers domicile, the form of motion to grant the prayer is simplified. If counsel avoids the issue in the petition, it may have to be dealt with by an unqualified solicitor's clerk at the counter of the petition department.

Signature of petitions

All petitions must be signed by counsel except (1) petitions for suspension, suspension and interdict, suspension and liberation and petitions under the Bankruptcy (Scotland) Act 1985 which may be signed by the petitioner's solicitor; and (2) a petitioner for the sequestration of his own estates who may sign the petition himself (rule 193). Certain applications to register a judgment under the Civil Jurisdiction and Judgments Act 1982 may be signed by the applicant (rule 249E (1); Form 58). Apart from these exceptions a layman who is intent on his own litigation needs the signature of counsel (*Gillies, Petr.*, P5/1/86, 2nd Division, January 17, 1986, unreported).

Answers should be signed by counsel (rule 28). It is common to find counsel signing papers on behalf of another counsel but it is not considered proper practice to do this in the instance of a paper which disposes of the merits of a petition, such as a joint minute or a minute of abandonment.

In *Marshall*, 1938 S.N. 18, the opinion was expressed that counsel should sign appendices containing facts which would form part of the petition but which were for convenience relegated to an appendix. Although this view was expressed in the course of hearing a petition for a *cy-près* scheme, the opinion was stated to apply to petitions generally. Observance of this rule has lapsed.

Caveats

In the first edition of this book we indicated that the practice was to accept *caveats* for (1) petitions for suspension, interdict, suspension and interdict and suspension and liberation (rule 236 (*b*); (2) a summons which includes a conclusion for interim interdict (rule 79); (3) petitions for sequestration; and (4) petitions for winding-up (rule 202 (*c*)). In *Kelly* v. *Monklands D.C.*, 1986 S.L.T. 165, Lord Ross held that a *caveat* might be lodged against an application for judicial review. He founded on a statement in Maxwell, *The Practice of the Court of Session* at p. 442, that a general *caveat* may be lodged against *any application* or there may be a particular *caveat* against a particular application. A similar view will be found in J. A. Maclaren, *Bill Chamber Practice*, p. 251.

The history of *caveats* is obscure. The earliest example which had been found of a procedure similar to *caveats* is in *Royal Bank of Scotland* v. *Bank of Scotland* (1729) 1 Paton 14, in which the Bank of Scotland obtained an opportunity to have warning of applications for letters of inhibition and arrestment (*cf. Wards* v. *Kelvin Tank Services Ltd.*, 1984 S.L.T. (Sh.Ct.) 39). In recent practice *caveats* have been limited to particular proceedings. Indeed a note to the styles in the *Encyclopaedia of Scottish Legal Styles*, Vol. 2, p. 322, suggests that at one time a *caveat* usually had to specify the name of the petitioner who might present a petition. The effect of Lord Ross's opinion in *Kelly* has been a reconsideration of the scope of *caveats*.

Although *caveats* have now been extended to include petitions for judicial review there is some reluctance by the petition department to extend *caveats* to any form of application (including motions) probably because of the administrative consequences, and, in some cases, the consequences for the petitioner. In theory *caveats* may apply to everything as diverse as adoption petitions, bills for letters of inhibition, the registration of a foreign judgment, an application under the Matrimonial Homes Act 1981 or the appointment of a judicial factor *ad interim* on the estate of a company. Whether it is wise to allow a respondent forewarning of these applications is a matter of policy which has yet to be fully discussed. There is a reluctance, at present, to accept a *caveat* for a custody petition or for a motion for interim custody. In petitions presented under section 1 of the Administration of Justice (Scotland) Act 1972 which seek an interim order for preservation of documents or productions without prior intimation to the respondent or haver, the present practice, when a *caveat* has been lodged, is for the clerk to take the petition, the motion for the interim order, and the *caveat* before a Lord Ordinary for a decision as to whether prior intimation of an application for an interim order should be made. *Caveats* against section 1 orders are accepted but they do not always result in notice to the *caveator*. The overall result is that the practice on *caveats* is fluid and confusing.

Caveats endure for 12 months. *Caveats* are always lodged in the petition department but the department sends a copy of any *caveat* which might be relevant to an action initiated by summons to the general department. The operation of *caveats* is explained at the appropriate point in the text.

Service and induciae

The normal rule is that after presentation of a petition with a process there is an order for such intimation, service and advertisement as may be necessary (rule 195). The exceptions to this are mentioned at the appropriate point in the text. Once the interlocutor has been signed, and the interlocutor sheet is available at the counter of the petition department, the interlocuor may be copied by the solicitor's clerk prior to service. Since an Act of Sederunt of May 31, 1978 (now rule 93A) it has been competent for a Depute Clerk of Session to write and sign an interlocutor (other than a final interlocutor) in respect of a motion which is not starred. This applies to a first order for intimation and service which is treated as if it had proceeded on a motion. It does not apply to Inner House cases.

There are now six *induciae* for petitions:

(a) four days. This applies to a petition under the Child Abduction and Custody Act 1985 (rule 260J (4)).

(b) eight days. This applies to petitions for winding-up (rule 218 (8)) and petitions to appoint a receiver (rule 215 (8));

(c) 14 days. This applies to certain petitions relating to judicial factors (rules 201 (*c*) and (*p*)) and to petitions for recall of sequestration (Bankruptcy (Scotland) Act 1985, s. 16 (2)). It is also relevant to sequestration petitions when the petition is presented by a creditor or a trustee acting under a trust deed (Bankruptcy (Scotland) Act 1985, s. 12 (12)).

(d) 21 days. Under rule 192 this is the normal *induciae* in a petition since January 1, 1987 for service within Europe and personal service outside Europe (see rule 192 (1) added by Act of Sederunt (Rules of Court Amendment No. 9) (Jurisdiction and Enforcement) 1986; S.I. 1986 No. 1941);

(e) 42 days. This applies to service outside Europe other than personal service (rule 192 (1));

(f) six months. This applies to edictal citation (rule 75 (7)).

The calculation of the *induciae* in postal service is reckoned from 24 hours after the date of posting (rule 192 (2)). Rule 195 applies to a petition the provisions of rules 74A, 74B and 75 on the citation and service of a summons. Rule 74A applies to citation within the United Kingdom. Rule 74B has elaborate provision on citation and service furth of the United Kingdom. Rule 75 applies to edictal citation. It used to be the case that citation of a person furth of Scotland required edictal citation. This is no longer the rule. After January 1, 1987 edictal citation was used only when the domicile of the party to be cited was unknown or the place where a person resided could not be ascertained or citation could not otherwise be effected. This rule was changed with effect from August 3, 1987 by the Act of Sederunt (Rules of Court Amendment No. 4) (Miscellaneous) 1987 (S.I. 1987 No. 1206). The present rule is that edictal citation is appropriate where the place where the defender resides cannot be ascertained or citation cannot be successfully effected in accordance with a method permitted under rule 74A (1) or 74B (1) (see rule 75 (1)).

A problem arises with personal service outside Scotland but within the United Kingdom. Rule 74A (4) provides for service by messenger-at-arms which is clearly incorrect. In practice solicitors should instruct the appropriate officer in other parts of the United Kingdom.

The first order in a petition follows the request for service in the prayer of the petition. If the facts turn out to be different, for example if a different address is found for the respondent, or the respondent's whereabouts cannot be discovered, it will be necessary to enrol a motion for amendment of the petition (and, if appropriate, for edictal service).

The *induciae* can be shortened on an application made by motion (rule 192 (3)).

Where a petition has been served on a respondent outside the United Kingdom under rule 74B and the whole or part of the prayer of the petition other than a procedural order has been granted without the respondent having lodged answers, intimation of a copy of the interlocutor must be made to the respondent who may, in certain circumstances, seek recall of the interlocutor and be allowed to lodge answers (rule 197).

The citation of service is regulated by Form 30 of the rules. A copy of the interlocutor which ordered service is appended to the copy petition and these are served with the citation. Where service by messenger-at-arms is required the interlocutor should be certified as a true copy by a clerk of court.

Intimation on the walls and in the minute book

The first interlocutor will usually order intimation on the walls and in the minute book. Intimation can be dispensed with (*Low*, 1920 S.C. 351; *Watson*, 1920 1 S.L.T. 243). No intimation on the walls or in the minute book takes place in adoption petitions or in petitions to apply judgments of the House of Lords. Intimation in the minute book only is ordered in petitions which relate to disciplinary matters involving solicitors.

Intimation on the walls is made by handing to the doorkeeper at the public entrance to Parliament House a copy of the details of the petition required by the *Practice Note* of November 16, 1961, which is printed in the *Parliament House Book.*

Intimation in the minute book is done by the clerks in the petition department. Generally speaking, the minute book contains abbreviated entries in longhand of first interlocutors and of decrees, which are treated as being interlocutors with the word "decerns." The minute book is required to be printed and published under rule 18. The Extractor's department print a weekly minute book which goes to the law libraries in the Parliament House complex, the Accountant of Court, the petition department and to others on a small and select circulation list. A yearly copy is bound and sent to the Keeper of the Records.

It will be noticed that the minute book does not contain a record of all the interlocutors of the court. The minute book is occasionally useful for tracing cases but whether this justifies the time and expense involved in maintaining it is questionable. One of the minor quirks of practice which seems designed to confuse the novice is that the walling certificate signed by the petitioner's solicitor or his clerk certifies that minuting has taken place although the solicitor has not been involved in, and has no control over, minuting.

Execution copy petition

An execution copy petition is lodged in process after the intimation, service and advertisement which were ordered. The execution copy petition is a *certified* copy of the petition to which an execution of service (Form 30) and a walling certificate (see Chapter 26) are attached (rule 195 (*d*)). Until the execution copy petition is lodged the petition department cannot check whether the *induciae* have expired.

Amendment of petitions

The practice in amendment of petitions is similar in Outer House and Inner House cases, except that in the latter case four copies of any minute and answers would be needed. The procedure can be examined in three situations:

(a) *Undefended petition.* Minor clerical amendments may be made without the necessity for a minute, *e.g.* a slight alteration to the designation of a party. A motion is enrolled to allow the amendment. It will normally be unstarred. On the motion being granted counsel initials the amendment or a solicitor may do so if he could competently sign the petition. For more complicated amendments a minute of amendment is lodged. A motion is enrolled to allow the petition to be amended in terms of the minute of amendment. Usually the motion will be unstarred. It may be necessary to obtain a warrant for re-service or service on new respondents.

(b) *Respondent in process, but no answers lodged.* This usually arises when a case is sisted. A motion will be enrolled on behalf of the petitioner to recall the sist and, if appropriate, to allow the petition to be amended in terms of the minute of amendment, or as the case may be, to allow minor amendments and of new to sist the cause. Usually this will be an unstarred motion. It is a common mistake to refer to answers to the minute in the motion, but answers to the minute are inappropriate when the respondent has not lodged answers to the petition.

(c) *Answers lodged.* If the petition and answers are at the preliminary stage before allowance of a hearing or proof (the order for which is approximately equivalent to the closure of a record in an ordinary action), amendment to the pleadings would be done normally by enrolling a motion for a period of adjustment of the petition and answers. In the case of a minor amendment, such as a change in the name or address of the parties, a motion could be enrolled to amend. After the allowance of a hearing or proof, the court would normally expect the parties to incorporate any further amendment to their pleadings into a minute of amendment, which, depending on the subject-matter, may or may not require answers. A party who receives intimation of a motion to amend can oppose the motion on the basis that he wishes to lodge answers. In the case of a major amendment the motion will anticipate the need for answers and seek to allow answers to the minute to be lodged within, usually, 14 days. Amendments to answers proceed *mutatis mutandis* as amendments to petitions. If a record has been printed the procedure is the same except, obviously, that it is the record and not the petition which is amended. The question may arise whether authority should be sought to reprint the record. Petitions for suspension, suspension and interdict and suspension and liberation are peculiar because they proceed like an ordinary action with an open record and a closed record. Accordingly it may be these documents which need to be amended. Amendment of pleadings when an interlocutor is being reclaimed raises special problems (see p. 22).

A new procedure was adopted for adjustment of minutes of amendment and answers by *Practice Note* of March 27, 1986. The procedure applies after an interlocutor which allows a minute of amendment to be received and answers to be lodged. Time limits are introduced to prevent undue delay. Twenty-eight days are allowed for adjustment. The period runs from the date answers are lodged (or the last set of answers lodged). On cause shown the period for adjustment may be extended. The party who has lodged a minute must enrol a motion to amend the record in terms of the minute or minute and answers. There is a 14-day period for enrolling this motion. The 14 days run from the expiry of the period of adjustment or, if no answers were lodged, from the last date for lodging answers. If the motion is not enrolled the court puts the case out for hearing in the by order roll and the court may make such order, including an order as to expenses, as it thinks fit.

Opposed petitions

Answers may be lodged at any time within the *induciae*. Answers may not be lodged although there is opposition to a sequestration petition (p. 128), an adoption petition (p. 34), or a petition for judicial review (p. 95). The court may, on cause shown, prorogate the time for lodging answers (rule 196 (*a*)). A request for prorogation may be made by motion which will not be starred in Outer House cases if the period is not excessive. It will be starred in Inner House cases. After answers have been lodged there may be a motion by either party to allow time to adjust the petition and answers. The authority of the court is needed for adjustment (rule 196 (*c*)). The adjustments are inserted on the principal petition and answers and initialled by counsel. In Inner House cases the adjustments should be made on the copy prints. After adjustment there may be a motion to print a record on the petition and answers as adjusted. Whether or not a print is necessary depends on the degree of adjustment and the ease with which the adjusted pleadings can be read without a record.

Petitions for suspension, suspension and interdict, and suspension and liberation, on answers being lodged, will normally have a motion to appoint the cause to the adjustment roll (rules 236 (*e*) and 245). Not later than seven days after the interlocutor which appoints the cause to the adjustment roll and caution or consignation, if ordered, has been found the petitioner must deliver six copies of an open record to the solicitor for each respondent and lodge two copies in process. The case then proceeds as an ordinary action (rule 247).

Disposal of motions

One of the principal matters raised in the Maxwell Report was the allocation of, and the time expended in the hearing of, motions (*Report of the Review Body on Use of Judicial Time in the Superior Courts in Scotland*, Scottish Courts Administration (1986), paras. 7.3 to 7.14). There were delays and disruption to the daily court programme because each judge in the Outer House was required to dispose of a number of motion roll hearings before commencing the substantive business of the day. "Starred" motions were dealt with by the appearance of counsel before the court. "Unstarred" motions were dealt with by a Depute Clerk of Session or by a judge in chambers without the attendance of counsel. The Maxwell Report recommended that Depute Clerks of Session should have a greater role in the disposal of motions and the result was a *Practice Note* of December 11, 1986 which allows for the disposal of unopposed motions under the following categories:

(1) Motions which according to previous practice were unstarred. These continue to be dealt with as unstarred motions.

(2) Motions of a procedural nature, which previously required the appearance of counsel, are dealt with by the clerk of court.

(3) Motions which require judicial consideration, and which previously required the appearance of counsel, are dealt with by a judge in chambers.

Illustrations of the types of motion in categories (2) and (3) were provided in two appendices to the *Practice Note*. The *Practice Note* also gives detailed information on the procedure for disposal of motions. The practice applies to Outer House motions only.

The clerks may refuse to accept a motion which *ex facie* is completely incompetent from a person who is not a party to the proceedings (*Rush* v. *Fife R.C.*, 1984 S.L.T. 390).

Motion to grant the prayer

Since August 3, 1987 there has been a new rule on the form of the motion to grant the prayer in an *unopposed* petition. This rule was added by the Act of Sederunt (Rules of Court Amendment No. 4) (Miscellaneous) 1987 (S.I. 1987 No. 1206). Rule 197 (*e*) states:

"A motion to grant the prayer of the petition shall state the ground of jurisdiction of the court and the domicile of the respondent (as determined by sections 41 to 46 of the Civil Jurisdiction and Judgments Act 1982) in so far as it is known to the petitioner."

If the petition has been drafted by counsel so that both jurisdiction and domicile are averred (see p. 6) the form of motion can be, "On behalf of the petitioner in respect that the court has jurisdiction in terms of paragraph X of the petition (and that the domicile of the respondent is stated in the said paragraph) to grant the prayer of the petition."

Rule 197 (e) has many difficulties and its terms need reconsideration. Most unopposed petitions do not have respondents. It cannot be the case that everyone on whom the petition is to be served is to be treated as a respondent whether or not they object to the petition. If there is no respondent it would appear unnecessary to refer to domicile but it remains to be seen how the practice of the petition department will develop. The domicile which may need to be referred to is not the "domicile" familiar to students of private international law. Domicile is defined in the sections of the 1982 Act referred to in the rule. Domicile is based on residence and connection with a country.

The major problem with rule 197 (e) is that it appears to be based on the erroneous assumption that the rules on jurisdiction in the Civil Jurisdiction and Judgments Act 1982 apply to most petitions. The converse is the case. The rules in the 1982 Act apply to very few petitions.

Jurisdiction under the 1982 Act

In summary the 1982 Act sets out three separate sets of rules on jurisidiction. These are:

(1) The 1968 Convention in Schedule 1. This applies when the defender is domiciled in another Contracting State (all EEC Member States except Ireland, Greece, Portugal and Spain, at the time of writing), or when the exclusive jurisdiction under article 16 applies.

(2) Schedule 4. This applies when the defender is domiciled in another part of the United Kingdom.

(3) Schedule 8. The Scottish rules apply when neither Schedule 1 nor 4 is applicable (note the primacy of the other Schedules. It is a mistake to assume that Schedule 8 contains all that a Scottish practitioner or court must consult). Normally Schedule 8 applies when the defender is domiciled in Scotland or in a country outwith the Contracting States (*e.g.* Spain or the U.S.A.)

The rules in Schedules 1, 4 and 8 all have exceptions. The 1968 Convention applies only in "civil and commercial matters" with certain exclusions (art. 1). Schedule 4 does not apply to the proceedings in Schedule 5. Schedule 8 does not apply to the proceedings in Schedule 9. When these exceptions are examined it will be found that they apply to most of the petitions listed in this book. The detailed references are given at the appropriate place in the text but a more general point is made by Schedule 9, paragraph 13 which excludes, from the Scottish rules, "proceedings which are not in substance proceedings in which a decree against any person is sought." On one interpretation this excludes almost all petitions (see A. E. Anton, *Civil Jurisdiction in Scotland* (1984), para. 10.8).

For further information on the 1982 Act see Anton, *sup. cit.* with a *Supplement*; R. Black, *Civil Jurisdiction; The New Rules* (1983); A. M., "The Civil Jurisdiction and Judgments Act 1982," 1987 S.L.T. (News) 29, which deals with the territorial scope of the Convention; and P. Beaumont, "European Court Case Law and Civil Jurisdiction in Scotland," 1987 S.L.T. (News) 201.

Intimation under certification

This procedure arises when a petitioner's solicitor ceases to act for his client or contact with the client is lost or, after answers have been lodged, when the respondent's solicitor has the same problem. The procedure is not appropriate or necessary for the respondent's solicitor before answers have been lodged.

The solicitor concerned writes a letter to the Deputy Principal Clerk of Session which intimates that the solicitor is ceasing to act for the client. The solicitor should send a similar letter to the agents for the other parties. The letter to the Deputy Principal Clerk is placed in process and given a process number. One of the other parties in the process enrols a motion.

> "On behalf of the petitioner/respondent in respect of the letter number —— of process, to ordain the respondent/ petitioner to intimate to the Deputy Principal Clerk of Session, 2 Parliament Square, Edinburgh within 14 days whether he intends to insist in his answers/petition, under certification that if he fails to do so the prayer of the petition shall be granted/refused."

The motion will be unstarred. A copy of the interlocutor is served by recorded delivery post. After the 14 days or other *induciae* have expired an execution of service is lodged with a backing as a separate part of process. Assuming that there has been no response to the intimation a motion may be enrolled for the desired order. An example of the procedure which involved failure to appear at the hearing of a reclaiming motion is *Spencer* v. *MacMillan's Tr.*, 1960 S.C. (H.L.) 84.

Consignation

The Accountant of Court receives consignation receipts for a variety of reasons including balances lodged under section 35 of the Judicial Factors Act 1849, and unclaimed dividends lodged in sequestrations under section 57 of the Bankruptcy (Scotland) Act 1985 and in liquidations under section 193 of the Insolvency Act 1986. Consignation sometimes arises in cases of recall of interdict or recall of an inhibition. The Accountant is sole custodier of consignations under the Court of Sessions Consignations (Scotland) Act 1895 (s. 3). Under section 2 the term "consignation" applies to any sum of money consigned or deposited in any bank under orders of the court, or in virtue of the provisions of any Act of Parliament.

When consignation is required by an Act of Parliament it may be that the consignation receipt is transmitted direct to the Accountant. When the consignation is the result of a court order a consignation receipt should be lodged in the process and it will be checked by the petition department clerk. A copy of the receipt is retained in the process and the principal receipt is transmitted to the Accountant (rule 13 (d)).

It is essential that all sums are lodged on a bank head office consignation receipt. A normal deposit receipt, even marked "consignation receipt" is unacceptable. The reason is the special nature of a consignation receipt. A partial upliftment may be made which facilitates the payment of portions of the sum to different parties. Deposit receipts receive simple interest, while consignation receipts receive compound interest under section 37 of the Judicial Factors Act 1849, a section which is not confined in its effect to factories.

A consignation receipt should be in the name of the Accountant of Court and his successors in office and should conclude with the words, "to await the further orders of the court." The procedure for claiming sums consigned in insolvencies is regulated by section 58 of the Bankruptcy (Scotland) Act 1985. Otherwise an order of court will be necessary before payment is made subject to the ability of the Secretary of State to make payment of small claims as detailed below.

After seven years the Accountant transmits consignation receipts to the Secretary of State for Scotland (Court of Session Consignations (Scotland) Act 1895, s. 9 as amended by the Transfer of Functions (Treasury and Secretary of State) Order, S.I. 1974 No. 1274). Where the Secretary of State is satisfied that any person has a legal right to any sum not exceeding £20, exclusive of interest, he may pay over that sum, without order of the court provided that competing claims have not been made (Law Reform (Miscellaneous Provisions) (Scotland) Act 1940, s. 6 (2) as amended by S.I. 1974 No. 1274).

In terms of rule 36, a certificate from the Inland Revenue that tax has been paid must be produced before there is an order for the payment of money consigned in the name of the Accountant or before a judicial factor is discharged unless the administration of the estate is continuing.

Certified copy interlocutors

Normally a party's solicitor makes up a copy of the order and this is certified by a petition department clerk. The exceptions to this are (a) an interlocutor which grants decree for interim aliment to which is appended a warrant for execution (rule 170 (*d*) (6)), (b) appointments of curators bonis and judicial factors and (c) interlocutors which approve trust variations under the Trusts (Scotland) Act 1961. In these exceptional cases the petition department prepare the certified copy interlocutors. In cases of interim variations of aliment orders following on a decree, an extract decree should be ordered and not a certified copy interlocutor.

Errors in interlocutors

An interlocutor pronounced by the court can, apart from the consent of the parties, be modified only if an application is made to the court *de recenti* (*Bruce* v. *Bruce*, 1945 S.C. 353). The alteration proposed must arise from a mistake of fact or clerical error or omission in the interlocutor (*Hutchison and Others, Petrs.*, 1965 S.L.T. 341; *Haberstich* v. *McCormick & Nicholson*, 1974 S.C. 241). Rule 30 (2) allows a judge who signs an interlocutor to correct or alter it at any time before extract, on cause shown. This has not been extended to an alteration designed to clarify an ambiguity in an interlocutor (*Davidson & Syme W. S.* v. *Booth*, 1971 S.L.T. (Notes) 11; sequel, 1972 S.C.1). An error in an extract decree can be corrected (*Mitchell's Trs.*, 1930 S.C. 180; *Provan's Trustee* v. *Provan*, 1987 S.L.T. 405).

Extraction of decrees

The issue of extracts is superintended by the Deputy Principal Clerk of Session who also holds the title of Principal Extractor of the Court of Session. The extracts are issued under his name. The form of extract is governed by rule 63 (inserted by Act of Sederunt (Rules of Court Amendment No. 8) (Miscellaneous) 1986; S.I. 1986 No. 1937).

To obtain an extract of an interlocutor a solicitor borrows the process from the petition department and takes it to the Extractor's office along with the transmission book kept in the petition department. The process and the transmission book are presented along with a note to the extractor. The note is headed with the designation of the parties followed by a copy of the interlocutor to be extracted and a request for the extract. The note is signed by the solicitor (see Extracts Department Regulations in the *Parliament House Book)*. In the Extractor's office a copy of the interlocutor in the note is compared with the principal and an entry made in the decreets book. The transmission book is returned to the petition department by the solicitor. An extract is prepared and the solicitor is informed by fee note. The process is returned to the petition department by court messenger with the decreets book. The decreets book is returned to the Extractor after the petition department clerk has acknowledged in it receipt of the process. In this way there is a record of the whereabouts of a process.

If the extract is final, that is, the last that can be issued in any process, the process is not returned to the petition department. Accordingly all productions such as medical certificates, trust deeds, or memoranda and articles of companies should be borrowed up prior to final extraction. Once there has been final extraction the process is marked "F" and it is stored eventually to be sent to the Scottish Record Office. Extracts are prepared in duplicate and a copy of an extracted decree can be made from this duplicate. After a short time the duplicates are sent to the Keeper of the Records and further extracts should then be ordered from the Scottish Record Office.

If the extract is interim there are still issues in the case which may have to be decided by the court. The process is not finished and it must be returned to the petition department.

> "The question whether extract is given *ad interim* or as final extract is, in my opinion, a question arising on the merits and not on the form of the application for extract. If something remains to be done in the process after extract, any extract given and taken must be assumed to have been given and taken *ad interim*" (*Smith* v. *Smith*, 1927 S.L.T. 462 at p. 462, *per* Lord Moncreiff).

Parties are not deprived of their rights by the erroneous issue of a final instead of an interim extract (*Brunt* v. *Brunt*, 1958 S.L.T. (Notes) 41).

Because final extract means that the process is at an end and cannot be brought before the court (except for the correction of clerical or accidental errors) it is important in some instances that the final interlocutor reserves the rights of parties to make further application to the court. This has the result that further applications can be made by motion or note in the process and need not be made by separate petition. In the present context this has a relevance to petitions for custody of children. Lord President Clyde expressed the point in this way;

> "[T]he effect of such a reservation . . . is that the 'final decree' so qualified is capable only of *interim* extract. The process is thus automatically preserved as a living process, in which future orders can be moved for under the reservation. If 'final decree' is pronounced *without reservation* . . . then, if extract is asked for, the extract is a *final* one, and the process is, so to speak, 'killed' and cannot be further moved in. Lastly, the 'final decree' may be allowed to remain unextracted. In that case the process to which it belongs becomes what is known as an 'unextracted process' . . . Such a process can generally be wakened (if necessary) and moved in for any competent purpose, but whether applications relative to the custody, maintenance, and education of the pupil children of the marriage can be competently made therein will depend on whether the final decree had a suitable reservation attached to it or not." (*Sanderson* v. *Sanderson*, 1921 S.C. 686 at pp. 692, 693).

The issue of an extract does not prevent review by the Inner House (rule 63B).

Report to the Inner House

Rule 198A provides that a Lord Ordinary may report a petition, or a matter arising in the course of a petition, to the Inner House for a ruling.

Reclaiming to the Inner House

The first problem facing a practitioner who wishes to reclaim is whether or not leave to reclaim is needed. Interlocutors in a winding up may be reclaimed without leave (Insolvency Act 1986, s. 375; rule 264 (*g*)). Leave is not required to reclaim against interlocutors which dispose of the whole or part of the merits of a case or granting, refusing, or recalling interim interdict or making an exclusion order under the Matrimonial Homes (Family Protection) (Scotland) Act 1981 and other types of interlocutors mentioned in rule 264 (*a*) and (*b*). In the case of a final interlocutor which contains an award of custody, access or aliment, the marking of a reclaiming motion does not excuse obedience to or implement of the award unless by order of the Lord Ordinary or one of the Divisions of the Inner House or of the Vacation Judge (rule 264 (*a*); see also rule 264 (*c*) when leave to reclaim is needed).

If leave of the Lord Ordinary is required rule 264 (*c*) applies. There is doubt about the interpretation of this rule. This arises because it may be necessary to enrol two motions, namely, a motion for leave to reclaim and, if leave is granted, a motion for review of the Lord Ordinary's interlocutor. The rule provides that the reclaiming must not be later than the seventh day "after the day on which the said interlocutor is pronounced." The difficulty is to decide which interlocutor this refers to. One view is that the seven days start to run from the interlocutor which grants leave to reclaim. The other view is that the period for reclaiming starts to run with the interlocutor to be reclaimed, with the consequence that two motions and two related interlocutors must occur within eight days. It is the latter view which is followed in practice. A further problem arises because the motion for leave to reclaim should be heard by the Lord Ordinary whose interlocutor is being reclaimed against. But that Lord Ordinary may be away on High Court duty. A motion for prorogation of the time for leave to reclaim should be enrolled. It is current practice to allow this motion to be heard by any Lord Ordinary.

If the leave of a Lord Ordinary is needed to reclaim, reclaiming does not excuse obedience to or implement of the interlocutor reclaimed unless the Lord Ordinary otherwise directs (rule 264 (*c*)).

To reclaim it is necessary to lodge 10 copies of a reclaiming print which consists of the pleadings and the interlocutors (rule 26 (*b*)). A motion in the style of Form 41 in the rules of court is enrolled. With effect from August 3, 1987 there is a procedure for lodging grounds of appeal (see rule 294B, added by the Act of Sederunt (Rules of Court Amendment No. 4) (Miscellaneous) 1987, S.I. 1987 No. 1206). Where a reclaiming motion has been enrolled the cause appears in the Single Bills for an order for the reclaimer or respondent to lodge grounds of appeal which must be lodged within 28 days. The grounds of appeal consist of brief specific numbered propositions. Failure to lodge the grounds means that a motion may be enrolled to refuse the reclaiming motion, but there is not any automatic refusal of the appeal. The grounds of appeal may be amended on cause shown. The person lodging grounds of appeal must intimate a copy to any other party and enrol for an order for a hearing. No specific provision is made in the rules for an extension of the 28-day period. One party may apply for a sist to make an application for legal aid and it is not clear how this would affect the running of the 28-day period (contrast the provisions for lodging an appendix in rule 294A (*a*)).

Until August 3, 1987 any reclaiming motion would normally have had the result that the cause would have been appointed to the summar roll except in a case of exceptional urgency, such as a reclaiming motion against an interim order, when the cause might be disposed of in single bills. This depended on the workload of the court and the estimated time of the hearing. Parties were advised to consult the Keeper of the Rolls for guidance. The major prerequisite to disposal of a motion on single bills was that the opinion of the Lord Ordinary must be before the Division before the merits of the case were heard. The introduction of rule 294B and the requirement for grounds of appeal to be lodged adds a major obstacle to the disposal of an urgent reclaiming motion. In certain cases there may be a strong argument in favour of dispensation with the terms of the rule.

When reclaiming becomes a serious consideration it is vital that the reclaimer's solicitor contacts the judge's clerk and requests a written opinion. Not only will a Division not hear a reclaiming motion without a written opinion from the Lord Ordinary but in fairness to both parties, and the Lord Ordinary, the application to the Lord Ordinary should be made while the matter is fresh in his mind. A particular problem arises with orders which vary custody, aliment or access. These may have been disposed of on a motion and, unless there was a detailed debate, the Lord Ordinary may not have retained detailed notes of the arguments which are often easy to forget. A failure to make an early request for a written opinion is a common oversight.

Within three months of appointing a cause to the summar roll an appendix must be lodged in terms of rule 294A. If this is forgotten the reclaiming motion is treated as abandoned (rule 294A (*b*). A motion to prorogate the time for lodging an appendix may be enrolled before the date on which the appendix is due to be lodged (rule 294A (*c*)). This motion may be heard by a Division or a vacation judge. Within seven days after a failure to comply with the three-month rule a motion may be enrolled to be reponed (rule 294A (*d*)) or the respondent may enrol a motion for leave to insist upon the appeal (rule 294A (*e*)). The court has a discretion to relieve parties from any failure to comply with the terms of rule 294A but it will do so only in exceptional circumstances (see *Comrie* v. *National Coal Board*, 1974 S.C. 237; *Haberstich* v. *McCormick & Nicholson*, 1974 S.C. 241).

Summar roll—amendment of pleadings

The function of the Inner House is principally that of an appeal court. It is reluctant to exercise its judgment when dealing with matters which have arisen for the first time on amendment to pleadings made after the decision of an inferior court. A *Practice Note* was issued on March 26, 1981. Although the *Practice Note* refers only to reclaiming motions from a Lord Ordinary it is applied to Sheriff Court appeals. The *Practice Note* states:

> "From time to time the result of the allowance of substantial amendment of pleadings in the course of reclaiming motions is that matters which have become of material importance in the action have not been the subject of consideration by the Lord Ordinary. Practitioners are reminded that in such circumstances the Inner House may think it desirable to require the case to be remitted to the Lord Ordinary for further hearing. In order that this possible course of action may be explored before reclaiming motions are put out for hearing any party enrolling a motion for a record to be amended in terms of a minute of amendment and any answers thereto should at the same time enrol for a direction as to further procedure."

By order roll (summar roll cases)

One of the factors which contributed to the misuse of court time and which was identified in the Maxwell Report was the late cancellation of diets in both Outer House and Inner House rolls (*Report of the Review Body on Use of Judicial Time in the Superior Courts in Scotland*, Scottish Courts Administration (1986), paras. 6.37–6.69). In an effort to minimise the consequences of late cancellation of diets in the summar roll a *Practice Note* of January 6, 1987 provides that all summar roll cases are put out by order not later than five weeks prior to the date on which the cause is to be heard on the summar roll. At the by order roll hearing parties are required (a) to advise the court whether or not the summar roll hearing is to proceed; and (b) the likely duration of any hearing. If the by order roll date falls within a vacation period, the hearing will be heard on a Tuesday by a vacation judge. The Keeper of the Rolls requires practitioners to provide him with the following information: (a) whether or not they are in a position to accept a diet at short notice; (b) the minimum notice required of a diet at short notice and (c) an assessment of the likely duration of the summar roll hearing. This procedure now provides a useful service to the court and litigants which enables the court to fix summar roll hearings which need urgent disposal. From August 3, 1987 the procedure has been supplemented by the new procedure in rule 294C for the fixing and allocation of diets.

Appeal to House of Lords

The Form of Appeal Directions as to Procedure and Standing Orders applicable to Civil Appeals are contained in the House of Lords Appeal Directions and Standing Orders which are in the *Parliament House Book*. Unless the time for appealing is limited by statute or by order of the House or of the court below, an appeal must be lodged in the House of Lords within three months of the date of the last order or interlocutor appealed from (Standing Order 1). This date is that on which the order or interlocutor was pronounced and not necessarily that on which it was entered, signed or issued (reg. 12 (i)). Provision is made for a petition for leave to present an appeal out of time owing to a misunderstanding or a technicality (reg. 12 (ii)).

An appeal to the House of Lords from a judgment of a Division of the Court of Session on the merits of a cause is competent except where appeal is excluded by statute. Interlocutory judgments can be appealed, however, only where (1) there was a difference of opinion amongst the judges of the Division or (2) leave to appeal is given by the Division (J. A. Maclaren, *Court of Session Practice*, p. 919; Standing Order XII).

An application for leave to appeal an interlocutory judgment can now be made by motion in the process and will normally be disposed of in single bills. If leave is granted by the Inner House the three-month time limit applies to the appeal and this period runs from the date of the interlocutor appealed from and not, from the date of the interlocutor which grants leave to appeal (see reg. 12 (i)).

On interim execution of an order when there is an appeal see *Lord Advocate* v. *Glasgow Corporation*, 1972 S.C. 287; sequel 1973 S.C. (H.L.) 1.

Expenses

Detailed consideration of the many problems of expenses is beyond the scope of this book. In outline, however, there are two types of findings of expenses although there are instances of special practices of which liquidation is the notable example. Normally expenses will be either (a) a finding out of a trust fund, curatory or other estate, or (b) a finding against a party. The interlocutor remits the account when lodged to the Auditor of Court for taxation. Unless there is a special reason for not doing so the court decerns against the party found liable in expenses as taxed by the Auditor (rule 348). The account is lodged in process and a copy of the account is intimated to each of the other parties to the cause. The full process is borrowed up and transmitted to the Auditor of Court's department for taxation. In curatories the procedure is different in that it is only necessary to borrow up a certified copy of the principal writ and the account. Objections may be made to the Auditor's taxation under rule 349 (2) and (3).

When an estate is being administered under the supervision of the Accountant of Court he checks the account before it is forwarded to the Auditor of Court. Otherwise the account is taken direct to the Auditor who taxes it.

CHAPTER 2

ADMINISTRATION ORDER

Introduction

The Insolvency Act 1986 introduced a new procedure which gives the court power to make an administration order (ss. 8 to 27). The reason for the procedure was to introduce a form of "company rescue" which was similar to receivership but which could apply even in the absence of a floating charge creditor who had power to appoint a receiver. The powers of an administrator in Schedule 1 to the Act are very similar to the powers of a Scottish receiver in Schedule 2. But the mode of appointment of an administrator is different from that of a receiver and the consequences of appointment of an administrator are very different from the effect of the appointment of a receiver (see T. Hughes, "Insolvency Administration—A New and Viable Alternative" (1987) 32 J.L.S. 268).

Jurisdiction

The court which has jurisdiction is the court which may wind up the company (Companies Act 1985, s. 744, applied by Insolvency Act 1986, s. 251). The winding up jurisdiction of the court is governed by sections 120 and 221 of the 1986 Act. The provisions of the Civil Jurisdiction and Judgments Act 1982 are excluded by the terms of article 1 of the 1968 Convention, Schedule 4 does not apply because of Schedule 5, para. 1 and Schedule 8 does not apply because of Schedule 9, para. 4.

The administration order

The court may make an administration order and appoint an administrator. The powers of the court are permissive and there is no requirement that an order must be made if the statutory provisions are complied with (s. 8 (1)). The court must be satisfied that the company is unable to pay its debts and that the making of the order will achieve one or more of four specified purposes (s. 8 (3)). An administration order cannot be made after a company has gone into liquidation (s. 8 (4)). The petition will be dismissed if there is a receiver of the company unless the court is satisfied of certain circumstances (s. 9 (3)). Notice of the petition has to be given to the floating charge holder who is entitled to appoint a receiver (s. 9 (2)). It is thought that in some cases the effect of intimation to the floating charge holder will be that he appoints a receiver. This is in part because if an administration order is made the floating charge creditor cannot then appoint a receiver and enforce his security (s. 11 (3)). If an administration order is made it prevents most creditors from enforcing their claims against the company (see s. 11 (3)).

The administration order appoints an administrator (s. 13). He manages the affairs and property of the company (ss. 14 to 17). The administrator makes proposals to a meeting of creditors (ss. 23 and 24). Further procedure depends on the creditors' reaction to these proposals.

The court has specific power to make interim orders (s. 9 (4) and (5)). On presentation of a petition the court may make an administration order *ad interim* and appoint an administrator *ad interim*.

Procedure

A petition for an administration order is an Outer House petition and it is governed by rules 209 to 213 (as amended by the Act of Sederunt (Rules of Court Amendment No. 11) (Companies) 1986; S.I. 1986 No. 2298). The procedure is regulated also by Part 2 of the Insolvency (Scotland) Rules 1986. Defects in procedure may be cured without a *nobile officium* petition under the provisions of section 63 of the Bankruptcy (Scotland) Act 1985 as applied by rule 7.32 of the Insolvency (Scotland) Rules 1986. Section 63 does not allow a radical change in the nature of the proceedings (see the annotations to s. 63 in *Current Law Statutes*).

In a simple case the procedure is

1. A petition is lodged with the other parts of a process. There will be also a copy of the petition for the Advocates' Library and an inventory of productions with productions. The petition may be presented by the company or the directors or a creditor (s. 9 (1)). The petition must have certain averments. There are nine points listed in rule 209 (3). The petition must state:

(1) the petitioner and the capacity in which he presents the petition, if other than the company;

(2) whether it is believed that the company is, or is likely to become, unable to pay its debts and the grounds of that belief;

(3) which of the purposes specified in section 8 (3) of the 1986 Act is expected to be achieved by the making of an administration order;

(4) the company's financial position, specifying (so far as known) assets and liabilities, including contingent and prospective liabilities;

(5) any security known or believed to be held by creditors of the company, whether in any case the security confers power on the holder to appoint a receiver, and whether a receiver has been appointed;

(6) so far as is known to the petitioner, whether any steps have been taken for the winding up of the company, giving details of them;

(7) other matters which, in the opinion of the petitioner, will assist the court in deciding whether to grant an administration order;

(8) whether a report has been prepared under rule 2.1 of the Insolvency Rules (independent report on affairs of the company), and, if not, an explanation why not; and

(9) the person proposed to be appointed as administrator, giving his name and address and whether he is qualified to act as an insolvency practitioner in relation to the company.

In addition it may be desired to specify why an interim administrator should be appointed including the purposes of that appointment in terms of section 8 (3). It is normal in insolvency matters for there to be some urgency. One of the issues which may give rise to difficulty is the requirement to lodge an independent report on the affairs of the company (rules 209 (3) (*h*) and 209 (4) (*b*)). If a report is not lodged there must be an explanation in the petition. In one of the earliest petitions presented the explanation was simply that there had not been enough time to prepare a report.

Assuming that an interim administration order is to be made and that an interim administrator is sought a motion will be enrolled for intimation, service and advertisement and for the interim order and appointment. The petition department clerk will check whether a *caveat* has been lodged (see p. 6; a procedure similar to that in a liquidation petition is followed; see p. 102). The motion need not appear in the Rolls of Court. The motion will go before a judge at the earliest convenient time. After hearing counsel an interlocutor may be signed in the following form:

"The Lord Ordinary having heard counsel Appoints the Petition to be intimated on the Walls and in the Minute Book in Common form; Appoints notice of the Petition to be given in terms of Rule 2.2 of the Insolvency (Scotland) Rules 1986 and grants warrant for service of the Petition, together with a copy of this interlocutor, upon the parties named and designed in the Schedule annexed to the Petition; Allows them, and all parties claiming an interest, to lodge answers, if so advised, within 21 days after such intimation, notice and service; meantime makes an administration order *ad interim* and Nominates and Appoints A (design) an insolvency practitioner, duly qualified under the Insolvency Act 1986, to be the administrator, *ad interim*, of [the company] for the purposes specified in section 8 (3) *(a)*, *(b)* and *(d)* of said Act; Appoints the clerk of court to give notice of this order forthwith to the said interim administrator; and Appoints the said interim administrator to advertise and give notice of this order forthwith in terms of rule 2.3 of the Insolvency (Scotland) Rules 1986."

The interlocutor may vary the purposes specified in section 8 (3). It has been known for the interlocutor specifically to give the interim administrator the powers in section 14 of and Schedule 1 to the Act. It is thought that this is unnecessary because the administrator *ad interim* is an administrator. He does not have specially restricted powers even although at a later stage the court may recall his appointment.

2. The petitioner's solicitor carries out intimation and service. The clerk of court intimates to the *interim* administrator who advertises in the *Edinburgh Gazette* and newspapers (see rule 2.3). The administrator also sends a certified copy of the order to the registrar of companies, and a copy to the Keeper of the Register of Inhibitions and Adjudications and to others listed in rule 2.3 (3). The procedure is untidy because some persons will receive both notice of the petition from the petitioner and notice from the administrator. At this stage one solicitor may act for both petitioner and *interim* administrator and it may be that he can arrange a suitable and efficient compliance with both rules 2.2 and 2.3. In any event it would assist the solicitor to draw up his or her own list of those who require notice or service or both of a particular petition. There is a difference between *notice* and *service*. The notice under rule 2.2 (1) is given on a statutory form (Form 2.1 (Scot)). The notice under rule 2.3 (3) is on Form 2.2 (Scot). The administrator may require several certified copies of the interlocutor to give notices under rule 2.3 (3). Some doubt arises as to whether, despite what has been said, the petitioner must serve on the persons listed in rule 2.2 (1). This doubt arises because of the terms of rule of court 210. This requires service of the petition, "unless the court otherwise directs." On one view this problem is solved by the standard form of interlocutor which does distinguish between notice under rule 2.2 and service on those names in the schedule to the petition. Those on whom service is effected must also have notice (rule 2.2 (2)).

If an interim order is recalled it is probable that the court will order notice and advertisement of the recall in terms of rule 2.3 (but possibly not notice which follows the scheme of rule 2.2). On recall the court would have to fix the remuneration of the interim administrator (rule 2.16). It will depend on the circumstances whether the expense of the interim administration is borne by the assets of the company or by the petitioner.

3. The petitioner's solicitor lodges an execution copy petition which will have evidence that all the required notice and service were effected. A motion is enrolled to grant the prayer of the petition. The motion should be unstarred. An interlocutor may be signed in the following form:

"The Lord Ordinary having considered the petition and proceedings, no answers having been lodged, makes an Administration Order in relation to [the company]; Nominates and Appoints A (design) an insolvency practitioner, duly qualified under the Insolvency Act 1986, to be the administrator of the said company, for the purposes specified in section 8 (3) *(a)*, *(b)* and *(d)* of the said Act; Appoints the clerk of court to give notice of this order forthwith to the said Administrator, and Appoints the said Administrator to advertise and give notice of this order forthwith in terms of Rule 2.3 of the Insolvency (Scotland) Rules 1986."

4. The clerk of court gives notice to the administrator who then carries out the procedure in rule 2.3. and gives notice to the company and creditors in terms of section 21 (1).

5. The administrator carries out the procedure to summon a meeting of creditors to consider his proposals (s. 21 and rules 2.4 to 2.13). A report of the meeting is sent to the Deputy Principal Clerk (rule of court 212). The report must have annexed to it details of the proposals which were considered by the meeting and of any modifications which were considered (rule 2.13). Where the report discloses that the meeting has declined to approve the administrator's proposals the cause will be put out "By Order" for determination by the insolvency judge of any order he may make under section 24 (5) of the Act (rule of court 212 (2)).

6. Various incidental applications and appeals are made by note in the process (rule of court 211). An abstract of receipts and payments is sent to the Deputy Principal Clerk every six months (rule 2.17 and rule of court 213 and Form 2.9 (Scot)). The administrator's remuneration is fixed by the creditors' committee (rule 2.16). If there is no creditors' committee the procedure to be followed probably will be similar to that which applies to a liquidator who does not have a liquidation committee.

7. Discharge or variation of the adminstration order is sought by lodging a note (rule of court 211 (1) (*d*) and see s. 18). There is a form for notice of the discharge to the registrar of companies (Form 2.4 (Scot)). Recall of an interim administrator would be sought by a motion.

CHAPTER 3

ADOPTION

Introduction
The statutory provisions relating to adoption are mainly to be found in the Adoption (Scotland) Act 1978 most of which came into force on September 1, 1984. The applicable rules of court are rules 219 to 230L. An excellent guide to the law is Sheriff Peter McNeill's *Adoption of Children in Scotland* (2nd ed., 1986).

Jurisdiction
Jurisdiction is governed by section 56 of the Adoption (Scotland) Act 1978. The Civil Jurisdiction and Judgments Act 1982 does not apply because article 1 of the 1968 Convention excludes questions of status of natural persons and Schedule 9, para. 1 excludes Schedule 8.

Petition for adoption
The types of adoption order are discussed by Sheriff McNeill (*op. cit.*, para. 1.03). There may be a petition for an adoption order (rule 222). The 1978 Act introduced a procedure for freeing a child for adoption. This disposes of the agreement of the natural parents in advance of an actual adoption (rule 220). (A former parent can apply to revoke the order by note in a petition for adoption (rule 221).) The adoption of a child abroad is governed by rule 223. These three types of adoption petition are Outer House petitions which have similar procedures.

A petition for a Convention adoption order is an Inner House petition (rule 230C). The "Convention" is the Convention on Jurisdiction, Applicable Law and Recognition of Decrees relating to Adoptions concluded at The Hague on November 15, 1965. Austria and Switzerland are the only countries which, so far, are Convention countries (Convention Adoption (Austria and Switzerland) (Scotland) Order 1978 (S.I. 1978 No. 1442)).

The majority of petitions relating to adoption are heard in the sheriff court but the Court of Session has exclusive jurisdiction if the child is not in Great Britain when the application is made or the application is for a Convention adoption order. For the purposes of illustration the procedure in the adoption petition under rule 222 is narrated below. This is the most common petition (although there are only three or four each year) and any other form of petition in the Court of Session is a rarity. All the Outer House petitions follow a similar procedure. Prior to the presentation of an adoption petition three months' notice must be given to the local authority within whose area the petitioners have their home unless the child was placed by an adoption agency (s. 22, 1978 Act). In certain circumstances a *nobile officium* petition has been granted to overcome the difficulties caused by a failure to give the three months' notice (P16/1/82, unreported).

In the simple case the procedure in a petition for adoption is as follows:

1. The petitioners lodge a petition which follows Form 36 (rule 222 (1)). Although it appears that it may be possible in the sheriff court for the petitioners to sign their own petition, this is not competent in the Court of Session (see p. 6; *cf.* McNeill, *op. cit.*, para. 5.07). Petitioners who wish to conceal their identity from natural parents or a guardian of the child may apply for a serial number to be assigned to the petition. The application is made in writing to the petition department (rule 222 (3)). Usually there is a relatively informal application made just before the petition is typed. The petition is then known as, for example, "Serial No. P1/3/87 for authority to adopt (name of child)." Whether or not a serial number is sought will largely depend on the attitude of the natural parents. It may be irresponsible not to seek a serial number if there is a prospect of abduction of the child or other violence. There should be lodged with the petition a copy of the petition for the Advocates' Library, a process and an inventory of productions with productions which must include the items listed in rule 222 (4). The petition department clerk checks, in particular, that the petition is in Form 36 and that the appropriate productions have been lodged. This takes a longer time than the initial check of most petitions.

2. An adoption petition is not intimated on the walls or in the minute book or advertised (rule 222 (2)). There is no service of the petition on potential respondents or an order calling for answers (see rule 222 (2); *cf.* McNeill, *op cit.*, para. 5.17). This prevents possible difficulties which might arise because the petition would reveal the names and address of the adopting parents to the natural parents and other details which should be concealed (see style of petition in Form 36). The notice of a hearing which will be given to the natural parents (Form 39C) deliberately gives little information. If a serial number is assigned to the petition, no information is given in Form 39C about the adopting parents.

3. The petition is taken before a Lord Ordinary in chambers. He

hears counsel. One of the matters which must be decided is whether the court will appoint a curator *ad litem*. In some cases a curator must be appointed; in other cases a curator may be appointed (rule 222 (5) (*c*) and (*d*)). The court must appoint a reporting officer who, in practice, is the same person as the curator *ad litem*, if any. The court must also order intimation to an adoption agency or a local authority (rule 222 (5) (*b*)). A typical form of interlocutor is:

> "The Lord Ordinary, having heard counsel, dispenses with the intimation of the petition on the walls and in the minute book; Appoints X advocate to be reporting officer and curator *ad litem* in terms of rule of court 222 (5) and she having appeared and taken the oath *de fideli administratione*, allows her to see the process; Appoints the petitioners to intimate a notice in Form 39B of the appendix to the rules of court, or as near as may be, to Y Regional Council and to lodge an execution of such service in process; Directs the petitioners to be liable for the fee of the reporting officer and curator *ad litem*."

4. An execution of service of Form 39B is lodged in process. Form 39B requires the local authority or adoption agency to submit a report with the contents stated in rule 222 (7). Three copies of the report are lodged in process and a copy sent to the reporting officer and curator (rule 222 (8)). The reporting officer's report must give the information required by rule 224 (2). The contents of the curator's report are in rule 224 (6). It helps the petition department clerks considerably if the reports follow the order of the relevant rules. The reporting officer may have difficulty complying with all the requirements of the rules, for example, if the child is illegitimate and the father cannot be contacted easily. If information cannot be obtained there should be an explanation. An incomplete report will probably result in a remit back from the court to prepare a further report. On the other hand perfection is not required and it must be borne in mind that there have been judicial strictures against delay in adoption petitions (*A. v. B. & C.*, 1971 S.C. (H.L.) 129; McNeill, *op. cit.*, para 5.03).

5. Three copies of reports by the reporting officer and curator *ad litem* are lodged in process (rule 222 (9) and (10)). Very difficult questions can arise if a party litigant wishes to see the process and all the reports. Rule 230 (6) provides that all documents lodged in process are open to the parties unless the court otherwise directs. But the practice is not to allow a party litigant immediate access to

all the papers in the process. The petition department errs on the side of caution because the interests of the child may be affected adversely and there may be factors unknown to the clerks. Anyone who is dissatisfied with this caution can argue his request before a Lord Ordinary.

6. Once the reports have been lodged the petition department informs the petitioners' solicitors (rule 222 (11)). A motion must be enrolled for a hearing within seven days. At this stage there would not normally be an order to cite witnesses and havers. There is no appearance before a Lord Ordinary unless a motion is enrolled which seeks an order under rule 222 (12). An interlocutor allows a hearing and appoints intimation of the hearing on Form 39C in terms of rule 222 (13). The date of the hearing is left blank in the interlocutor and the petitioners' solicitors fix a date with the Keeper of the Rolls.

7. Although no order for answers will be made in the normal case a person who opposes the petition may lodge answers at some stage. In some cases there has been adjustment of the pleadings and the printing of a record. But it is thought that this is incorrect procedure. Rule 196 which governs the lodging of answers and adjustment does not apply to an adoption petition (rule 222 (2)). Answers, if tendered, will be accepted into the process but the hearing should normally take place without an adjustment of pleadings. There may be a sist to allow a party to apply for legal aid. There may be an application for an interim order (rule 222 (15)); s. 25, 1978 Act).

8. At the hearing, which will be in chambers, the petitioners will be represented by counsel. Other parties may appear (rule 222 (14)). The curator and reporter does not normally appear unless there is a problem with the reports. The court could make a custody order (Children Act 1975, s. 53). Where the same evidence applies to more than one petition the appropriate procedure is for the judge to hear parties on each of the petitions separately and to issue an interlocutor in each case (*A.B.* v. *C.B.*, 1985 S.L.T. 514). If the petition is granted an interlocutor is passed in the form:

> "The Lord Ordinary having heard counsel authorises the petitioners A and B to adopt the male child —— who was born in (country) on (date) and is identical with (name) to whom an entry numbered —— and made on (date) in the Register of Births for the Registration District of —— relates, in terms of the Adoption (Scotland) Act 1978; Directs the Registrar General for Scotland to make an entry recording said Adoption in the Adopted Children Register giving —— as

the Christian names and —— as the surname of the said adopted child, and to include the above mentioned date and country of birth in the entry recording adoption: and Directs the said Registrar General to cause the entry of the birth of said child in the Register of Births to be marked with the word 'Adopted.' The (agency) has taken part in the arrangements for placing the said child in the care of the petitioners. Relationship of petitioners to child —— ."

9. A certified copy of the order is communicated to the Registrar General by the clerk of court. The clerk sends the copy order by personal delivery in a sealed envelope marked "confidential" (rule 229). The order can be extracted only following on a petition to the court (rule 230 (3)). After transmission to the Registrar General the process is placed in a sealed envelope and kept in a secure place in the petition department. The envelope cannot be opened for 100 years except in limited circumstances which include the application of the adopted child who has reached the age of 17 (rule 230 (4)). At some stage the process will be transferred from the petition department to the Scottish Record Office.

Confidentiality
It is worth emphasising the confidential nature of the proceedings in adoption. From time to time solicitors make requests to examine an adoption process. But only the persons who are listed in rule 230 (6) may inspect the documents while the case is in progress. Even so access may, in the first instance, be denied to a party litigant (see para. 5 of the procedure noted above) and solicitors are expected to be sensitive to the reasons why disclosure of information can be harmful. Sometimes there is disclosure to a solicitor with a request that his client should not be told. A local authority or an adoption agency cannot see the process (see rule 230 (6) (*a*)). After an adoption order has been communicated to the Registrar General the 100-year rule applies (see above) and even the solicitors for the petitioners cannot examine the process without an order of court.

CHAPTER 4

ARBITRATION

Introduction

The only specific mentions of arbitration in the rules of court relate to the registration of awards under the Arbitration (International Investment Disputes) Act 1966 (rule 249A) and the procedure for a stated case (rules 276 to 280). But two other matters are sometimes brought to the court, namely, a petition to appoint an arbiter and a petition which seeks authority to cite witnesses or produce documents. Both petitions are Outer House petitions and the procedure is detailed below.

The Court of Session may order an arbiter to proceed (*Forbes* v. *Underwood* (1886) 13 R. 465) but it has been held that in a situation of any complexity a petition is not the correct procedure (*Watson* v. *Robertson* (1895) 22 R. 362). It has been suggested that, in certain circumstances, judicial review (Chapter 14) may be the appropriate method to review arbitration proceedings (see "Administrative Law," in *Stair Memorial Encyclopaedia*, Vol. 1, paras. 348–400).

Jurisdiction

In the Civil Jurisdiction and Judgments Act 1982 arbitration is excluded from the scope of the 1968 Convention (Sched. 1, art. 1). Rule 2 (13) of Schedule 8 provides that the Court of Session has jurisdiction in proceedings concerning an arbitration which is conducted in Scotland or in which the procedure is governed by Scots law. (See on the application of these rules, A. E. Anton, *Civil Jurisdiction in Scotland* (1984), paras. 3.23–3.26 and 10.48–10.50.)

Appointment of arbiter

The authority of the court to appoint an arbiter is in sections 2, 3 and 6 of the Arbitration (Scotland) Act 1894. Under these sections the court has no power to appoint an arbiter if the dispute is referred to arbitration without specification as to the number of arbiters *(McMillan & Son Ltd.* v. *Rowan & Co.* (1903) 5 F. 317). In such a case it may be that the remedy is a *nobile officium* petition. Procedure by way of petition may be inappropriate if the court is asked to decide complicated questions on, say, jurisdiction or the existence and construction of an arbitration clause (*Cooper*

& *Co.* v. *Jessop Bros.*, 1906 8 F. 714; *United Creameries Co. Ltd.*
v. *Boyd & Co.,* 1912 S.C. 617).

The procedure under the 1894 Act is simple in the case of an
unopposed petition. A petition is lodged with a copy for the
Advocates' Library, a process and an inventory of productions
with productions which will include the arbitration agreement.
The prayer of the petition seeks intimation and service and the
appointment of a named person as arbiter. An interlocutor orders
intimation and service. If no answers are lodged within the
induciae, after an execution copy petition is lodged a motion is
enrolled to grant the prayer of the petition. The prayer of the
petition will be granted and the arbiter appointed.

To cite witnesses and havers

The authority of the court can be sought to compel a witness to
attend a proof in an arbitration or to produce a document. The
petition seeks authority to cite witnesses and havers or appoint a
commissioner, as appropriate. (See *Crudens Ltd., Petrs.*, 1971
S.C. 64, which, for some reason, proceeded as an Inner House
petition. Petitions of this nature are not now as rare as that case
might suggest.) The petition usually narrates that the arbiter has
signed an interlocutor which the respondent refuses to comply
with. The arbiter should be asked to approve any specification of
documents. The petition is lodged with a copy for the Advocates'
Library, a process and an inventory of productions with productions. The petition is unusual in that it may proceed without
intimation or service. After considering the motion the Lord
Ordinary may grant warrant to messengers-at-arms, sheriff officers and the petitioner's solicitors to cite witnesses and havers. If a
commission is sought the interlocutor would be in the form:

> "The Lord Ordinary having considered the petition and
> proceedings, no *caveat* having been lodged, dispenses with
> intimation, service and publication in terms of Rule of Court
> 195 (*a*); grants diligence for citing havers; grants commission
> to —— to take the oath and examination of the havers
> required by the specification of documents granted by the
> arbiter on [date] and to receive their exhibits and productions."

If a witness who was cited refused to attend, evidence of the
citation would be lodged in process and a motion enrolled, "On
behalf of the petitioner to grant letters of second diligence against
A (design) in respect of his refusal to attend the arbitration on
[date] to which he has been duly cited." An interlocutor would
grant authority to the clerk of court to issue letters of second
diligence.

As it is difficult to find authority which deals with letters of second diligence the following quotation from Erskine (*Inst.*, IV. ii. 30) may help to elucidate matters;

> "[W]here a witness does not appear on the date fixed by the warrant of citation, a second warrant is granted, called letters of second diligence, which is of the nature of a caption, and contains a command to the messenger whose name is filled up in the warrant, to apprehend him, and bring him before the court. If the witness answers on the first warrant, he is entitled to his expense from the party who cites him, which is ascertained at a certain rate *per diem*, as he travels on horseback or walks a-foot; but if the party is put to the trouble of obtaining a second diligence, the witness must bear his own charges."

The letters of second diligence, in modern practice, give authority to messengers-at-arms and sheriff officers to search for and apprehend the witness and to place him in captivity until he finds sufficient caution to appear before the arbiter. The letters are signeted.

Evidence to lie in retentis

It may be sought to take evidence on commission before a proof in an arbitration can be heard or even, in exceptional circumstances, before the arbitration has commenced. The reason might be that a witness is frail and unlikely to live until the expected date of the proof. The remedy is an Inner House petition to the *nobile officium* for a commission to take the evidence (*Galloway Water Power Co.* v. *Carmichael*, 1937 S.C. 135). After the commission is executed the shorthand notes of the evidence are lodged in the process to await the further orders of the court. Further orders may be sought by a motion or note in the process.

CHAPTER 5

CHILD ABDUCTION

Introduction

Child abduction is a criminal offence both at common law and under section 6 of the Child Abduction Act 1984. Under section 51 of the Children Act 1975 it is an offence to remove a child without authority from a person who has applied for custody of the child and who has had care and possession of the child for three years. A court may order the return of the child (s. 52).

The civil remedies for child abduction are to seek delivery of the child and, where appropriate, interdict. These orders may be sought in a petition for custody (see Chapter 6) or in a separate petition. For example in *Campbell* v. *Campbell*, 1977 S.C. 103 a wife who held an order for custody from a Texas court discovered that her husband and children were in Scotland. She petitioned the Court of Session for custody, delivery and interdict. On an *ex parte* application the court granted authority to messengers-at-arms to search for and uplift the children. Thereafter answers were lodged by the husband but the prayer of the petition was granted without a proof. In *Thomson, Petr.*, 1980 S.L.T. (Notes) 29 the issue of custody had not been decided by an Australian court and Lord Stott ordered delivery of the child to the petitioner but made no award on custody.

The international aspects of child abduction continue to give rise to problems. The temptation for the parent without custody is to abduct the child and move with the child to a foreign country. The hope is that the whereabouts of the child may be concealed, at least for a while. When the matter is brought before a foreign court the argument will be that it is in the best interests of the child to keep the child in the surroundings to which the child is now accustomed. The parent from whom the child was abducted faces formidable problems. The Child Abduction and Custody Act 1985 was passed to assist the return of abducted children. The Act gives effect to a Hague Convention (on which see A. E. Anton (1981) 30 I.C.L.Q. 537) and to a European Convention (on which see R. L. Jones (1981) 30 I.C.L.Q. 467). These conventions deal with the recognition and enforcement of foreign custody orders.

A custody order made by a court in any part of the United Kingdom will be recognised in Scotland under section 25 of the Family Law Act 1986. The custody order may be registered (s. 27) and enforced (s. 29).

Jurisdiction in an action for delivery is regulated by section 17 of the Family Law Act 1986. Actions relating to the custody of children are excluded from the jurisdiction rules under the Civil Jurisdiction and Judgments Act 1982 because they are classified as actions relating to status. See A. E. Anton, *Civil Jurisdiction in Scotland* (1984), para. 3.14; Sched, 1, art. 1 and Sched. 9, para. 2 of the 1982 Act.

Procedure

A petition for delivery is often combined with a claim for custody, although a petition for delivery alone would be competent if the petitioner had a *prima facie* entitlement to custody (see E. M. Clive, *Husband and Wife* (2nd ed.), p. 546). If custody and delivery are sought the procedure will follow that for a custody petition (see Chapter 6). If delivery alone is sought it would not be necessary to have the extensive intimations required of a custody petition. In either case there may be an interim order for delivery which can be sought on an *ex parte* motion. It may be that the whereabouts of the children are unknown in which case it is necessary to seek an order to trace the children. The interlocutor may be in the form:

> "Grants warrant to and authorises messengers-at-arms and sheriff officers to search for the persons of said children and report to the court on their whereabouts; Requires all sheriffs in Scotland to grant their aid in the execution of such warrant and recommends all competent courts in the United Kingdom and elsewhere to give their aid and concurrence therein; Authorises execution of this order to proceed upon a certified copy of this interlocutor."

Neither procurators fiscal nor the police have a duty to assist in the search for children under an interlocutor for delivery (*Caldwell* v. *Caldwell*, 1983 S.C. 137, which settled the form of interlocutor). The court could grant a commission to take evidence from witnesses who might know where the children are (*Abusaif* v. *Abusaif*, 1984 S.L.T. 90 which doubts *Caldwell, sup. cit.,* on this point). A power to order disclosure of a child's whereabouts in custody proceedings is conferred by section 33 of the Family Law Act 1986.

When it is sought to enforce an order under the Child Abduction and Custody Act 1985 the procedure followed is in rules 260H to 260L. The rules regulate the content of the petition, the productions which accompany it, the *induciae* (four days), and the persons on whom the petition must be served. Recent examples of petitions under the 1985 Act are *Kilgour* v. *Kilgour*, 1987 S.C.L.R. 344 and *Viola, Petr.*, 1987 S.C.L.R. 529.

Enforcement of a custody order under the Family Law Act 1986 will be governed by rules of court which, at the time of writing, had not been made.

CHAPTER 6

CHILD CUSTODY

Introduction

The statutory provisions which regulate the custody of children are primarily the Children Act 1975 (the "1975 Act"), sections 47 to 55, the Law Reform (Parent and Child) (Scotland) Act 1986 (the "1986 Act") and the Family Law Act 1986. Rules of Court 260C to 260E detail the procedure in a petition for custody. These rules were added by Act of Sederunt (Rules of Court Amendment No. 2) (Custody of Children) 1986; S.I. 1986 No. 515. It is expected that rules will be made under the Family Law Act 1986 (when the Act is in force).

Who may present a petition?

Section 3 (1) of the 1986 Act provides:

> "Any person claiming interest may make an application to the court for an order relating to parental rights and the court may make such order relating to parental rights as it thinks fit."

The reference to "any person" should be noted. The petitioner, for example, may be a relative of the child, a foster parent, or a natural parent who wishes exclusive custody. (But see a restriction discussed in J. M. Thomson, "Applications for Parental Rights," 1987 S.L.T. (News) 165.) The petition may be brought for "an order relating to parental rights." This means an order for tutory, curatory, custody or access, and any right or authority relating to the welfare or upbringing of a child conferred on a parent by any rule of law (1986 Act, s. 8). This chapter is concerned with custody and access. Tutory and curatory are mentioned at pp. 76, 88 and 119 and child abduction in Chapter 5.

Jurisdiction

The court may entertain a petition for a custody order only if it has jurisdiction under section 9, 10, 12 or 15 (2) of the Family Law Act 1986. Section 9 relates to the habitual residence of the child in Scotland; section 10 is concerned with a child who is present in Scotland but not habitually resident in any part of the United Kingdom; section 12 confers an emergency jurisdiction when the child is present in Scotland; and section 15 (2) gives power to vary or recall an order notwithstanding that the court would no longer have jurisdiction to make the original order.

Actions relating to the custody of children are excluded from the jurisdiction rules under the Civil Jurisdiction and Judgments Act 1982 because they are classified as actions relating to status. See A. E. Anton, *Civil Jurisdiction in Scotland* (1984), para. 3.14; Sched. 1, art. 1 and Sched. 9, para. 2. of the 1982 Act.

Intimation of the petition

One of the features of the 1975 Act, the Law Reform (Parent and Child) (Scotland) Act 1986 (the "1986 Act") and rule 260D is that intimation of the petition may have to be made to a wide variety of people. The rules are complex and although an attempt is made to summarise them here, there is no adequate substitute for a study of the actual words.

Section 48 (1) of the 1975 Act provides that so far as practicable notice of an application for custody must be given to each known parent of the child. The father of an illegitimate child is a parent. Section 49 of the 1975 Act as amended by the 1986 Act states that where an applicant for custody is not a parent notice of the application must be given to a local authority. Cause can be shown for not giving notice. The section regulates the time for giving notice and the local authority to which it is to be given.

Rule 260D reinforces the statutory provisions. Form 53 is sent to each known parent. Form 55 is sent to the local authority. (It is expected that rule 260D will be amended to make it coincide with the alterations to s. 49 of the 1975 Act which were made by the 1986 Act.)

Consent to the custody order

Certain consents may be needed if the petitioner is not a parent, tutor, curator or guardian of the child (s. 47 (2), 1975 Act as amended by the 1986 Act). No consent is needed if the petitioner has had care and possession of the child for three years, including the three months preceding the petition. Otherwise a relative or step-parent of the child needs the consent of a parent, tutor, curator or guardian and the petitioner must have had care and possession for three months prior to the petition. Other petitioners need the same consent but the qualifying period for care and possession is 12 months including the three months preceding the petition. The consent is given on Form 54 in all cases even although rule 260D, as at present drafted, does not deal with an application by a person other than a relative, step-parent, or foster parent.

Procedure

Any petition for the custody of children brought under an Act or at common law is an Outer House petition (rule 189 (*a*) (xx)). At common law all applications for custody were applications to the *nobile officium*, but now all these cases are presented in the Outer House (*Syme* v. *Cunningham,* 1973 S.L.T. (Notes) 40).

1. The petition is presented with a copy for the Advocates' Library, a process, an inventory of productions and productions such as marriage and birth certificates.

2. A motion may be enrolled for interim interdict and interim custody. An order may also be sought for delivery or tracing of the child (see p. 40). The order for intimation and service must require that the petitioner gives notice on Forms 53 to 55, as appropriate. The interlocutor will specify the time limits for giving the notices. In the case of an applicant who is resident in Scotland, and who is not a parent, the notice to the local authority must be given within seven days following the presentation of the petition or the order for custody cannot be made except on cause shown (s. 49, 1975 Act, as amended by the 1986 Act; rule 260D (2) (*b*)).

3. An execution copy petition and any consents required are lodged. Where a petitioner is not a parent the local authority prepares a report under section 49 of the 1975 Act as amended by the 1986 Act and lodges three copies of the report in process (rule 260D (6)) (and sends a copy to the curator *ad litem,* if any).

4. The court may have appointed a curator *ad litem* (but does not normally do so). The curator reports on the matters listed in rule 260D (5). The curator lodges three copies of his report in the process.

5. On receipt of all the reports the petition department informs the petitioner and makes the reports available (rule 260D (8)). If no answers have been lodged a motion is enrolled to grant the prayer of the petition and for expenses. The motion is dealt with by a judge in chambers. The interlocutor will be in approximately the following form:

> "The Lord Ordinary having considered the petition and proceedings, no Answers having been lodged, and having heard counsel, finds the petitioner entitled to the custody of the children—and decerns against the respondent for payment to the petitioner of the sum of £X sterling per week as aliment for each of the said children while in the custody of the petitioner and unable to earn a livelihood. Reserves leave to any person claiming an interest to apply to the Court in this

process until [date] for any further order that may be required regarding custody and aliment; finds the respondent liable to the petitioner in expenses and remits the account thereof, when lodged, to the Auditor of Court to tax and report."

There may be two reservation dates in the interlocutor. Leave to apply on custody is reserved until the youngest child attains 16 and for aliment until that child attains 18. The reason for the rule on aliment is the provisions of section 1 of the Family Law (Scotland) Act 1985. It has not always been the practice of counsel when drafting custody petitions to include two reservation dates in the prayer but, in an appropriate case, it would be good practice to do so.

The reservation of leave to apply to the court prevents extraction of this interlocutor being a final extraction (see p. 19). If this reservation was not in the interlocutor any further application to the court would have to be by way of petition. If use is made of the reservation to vary custody the procedure is by minute lodged in process and served on the other party. Variation of aliment or access proceeds on a motion and should follow the procedure set out in rule 170B (10).

6. If answers are lodged the procedure is similar to a normal opposed petition (see p. 12). In a dispute on access the Second Division decided that proof should take place in open court and an interview of the child by a Lord Ordinary was an undesirable substitute for a proof (*MacDonald* v. *MacDonald*, 1985 S.L.T. 244).

7. In terms of the *Practice Note* of November 13, 1969, motions for interim custody and for interim aliment, or for a variation of interim custody, require a seven-day intimation to the other side except in the case of special urgency when the normal 48 hours' intimation applies. The *Practice Note* does not cover interim access motions which are governed by the normal rules for intimation of motions (rule 93). A motion for variation or recall of aliment or interim aliment or access requires a 14-day *induciae* and the special provisions of rule 170B (10) apply.

8. Prior to the present rules the court had a practice in some cases of remitting to a reporter. Although this could still be done, the curator *ad litem* appointed in terms of rule 260D (4) and (5) can perform most of the functions of a reporter.

CHAPTER 7

COMMISSION AND DILIGENCE

Introduction

An application for commission and diligence which is made in a cause before or after calling is regulated by rules 95 and 95A. This chapter is concerned with the petition procedure which arises as a result of rule 95A (*c*). That rule applies where proceedings have not commenced and it is sought to have an order under section 1 of the Administration of Justice (Scotland) Act 1972. These petitions are relatively common and are often described as "section 1" petitions.

Section 1 of the 1972 Act empowers the court to order inspection, production and recovery of documents and other property which might be used in court proceedings. As amended the section gives the court power to order disclosure of the identity of potential witnesses and defenders (Law Reform (Miscellaneous) Provisions) (Scotland) Act 1985, s. 19; and see rule 95A (*d*) as substituted by the Act of Sederunt (Rules of Court Amendment No. 4) (Miscellaneous) 1987; S.I. 1987 No. 1206). Section 1 also allows a variety of other orders to be made and it has been used to obtain photographs of the site of an accident and to allow an expert to carry out tests on machinery.

One of the benefits of section 1 is that the court may make an order when the petition is presented and before it is served. The competence of making an order on an *ex parte* statement was settled in *British Phonographic Industry Ltd.* v. *Cohen, Cohen, Kelly, Cohen & Cohen Ltd.*, 1983 S.L.T. 137. The court appoints a commissioner who goes to the premises of the respondent with messengers-at-arms and the petitioner's solicitor. The order and the petition are served on the respondent and the commissioner then attempts to recover the property. In this way there is an element of surprise and the respondent may not have time to destroy evidence. The property is removed to the custody of the Deputy Principal Clerk of Session who preserves the property on behalf of the court. Unfortunately the items recovered may remain in the court and it is believed that in the vaults of the Court of Session there is a considerable collection of pirated video tapes. On the other hand the petitioner may seek to uplift the items recovered. In this way it has been known for a petitioner to regain possession of his own property. This may not have been the intention of section 1, and it may not always be allowed, but it is interesting that this method of recovery of property does not find favour with those who seek to enforce a retention of title clause.

One of the difficulties with section 1 is that an order is subject to the privilege against self-incrimination (see *British Phonographic Industry Ltd., sup. cit.*). This privilege has now been withdrawn in certain proceedings relating to intellectual property (Law Reform (Miscellaneous Provisions) (Scotland) Act 1985, s. 15). This removes a major obstacle to the use of section 1 in copyright infringement cases.

A section 1 petition is competent where proceedings "are likely to be brought" in which the applicant will be a party or minuter. There must be an intelligible *prima facie* case before the petition will be granted (*Moore* v. *Greater Glasgow Health Board*, 1978 S.C. 123; *Thorne* v. *Strathclyde R.C.*, 1984 S.L.T. 161; *Smith, Petr.*, 1985 S.L.T. 461). The property to be recovered must relate to a dispute which might relevantly arise (*Micosta S.A.* v. *Shetland Islands Council,* 1983 S.L.T. 483).

Not every petition under section 1 seeks an immediate appointment of a commissioner. Sometimes the petitioner is content to serve the petition and wait and see if answers are lodged. This is especially appropriate if the petition is seeking an order which allows experiments or inspection of machinery to be carried out (on the averments needed see *Thorne* v. *Strathclyde R.C.*, 1984 S.L.T. 161). It is also the practice to serve on the Lord Advocate when a government department or state hospital is involved.

Jurisdiction

Section 1 of the 1972 Act applies to proceedings which are likely to be brought before the Court of Session. The power of the Court of Session is extended by section 28 of the Civil Jurisdiction and Judgments Act 1982 to cover proceedings which may be brought in another Contracting State or in the rest of the United Kingdom.

Procedure

The procedure in a petition which seeks an immediate appointment of a commissioner is as follows:

1. The petition is lodged with a copy for the Advocates' Library, and a process. The petition must specify the matters in respect of which information is sought of persons who might be witnesses or defenders (rule 95A as substituted by the Act of Sederunt (Rules of Court Amendment No. 4) (Miscellaneous) 1987; S.I. 1987 No. 1206). The petition department check whether a *caveat* has been lodged. According to present practice within the petition depart-

ment the existence of a *caveat* will not necessarily give the caveator a right of intimation at this stage. A clerk places the process and the *caveat* before a Lord Ordinary in chambers so that a decision may be made as to whether or not notice to the caveator is appropriate in the circumstances of the case. The prayer of the petition will seek intimation and service and order appointing a commissioner. A motion is enrolled. "On behalf of the petitioner to appoint a Commissioner in terms of the prayer of the petition and for warrant for intimation and service." The petitioner sometimes also seeks interim interdict. Counsel appears before a Lord Ordinary and argues for the commissioner's appointment. An interlocutor may be signed which states:

> "The Lord Ordinary appoints the petition to be intimated on the Walls and in the Minute Book in common form, and to be served as craved along with a copy of this interlocutor; allows all parties claiming an interest to lodge Answers thereto, if so advised, within fourteen days after such intimation and service; having heard counsel and no caveat having been lodged appoints X advocate to be the Commissioner of the Court therein and grants warrant to and authorises the said Commissioner to take all steps which he may consider necessary to search for, identify and recover and take possession of [details of property] and convey same to the Deputy Principal Clerk of Session, 2 Parliament Square, Edinburgh, to await the further orders of the Court and decerns."

2. A certified copy of the interlocutor is needed to execute the commission. The messenger-at-arms will also insist on a certified copy if an interim interdict has to be served (see p. 144). Arrangements are made with the commissioner to execute the commission. The commissioner receives the certified copy of the interlocutor and appoints a shorthand writer as clerk and administers to him the oath *de fideli administratione officii*. The commissioner goes to the premises where the property is thought to be. He is accompanied by his clerk, the petitioner's solicitor, and a messenger-at-arms and the messenger's witness. The petition and the first order are served by the messenger-at-arms and the commissioner attempts to trace and recover the relevant property. The property is lodged with the Deputy Principal Clerk of Session and the commissioner lodges in process a copy of his report and an inventory of the items recovered.

3. The property is not recovered directly by the petitioner. It is recovered "to await the further orders of the Court." If the

petitioner wishes to uplift the property a motion is enrolled, "On behalf of the petitioner to uplift the productions recovered by way of Commission." The respondent, who by this time might have lodged answers to the petition, could enrol a motion for redelivery of the items. Either party may be required to find caution (rule 95A (c)).

4. The respondent may object to recovery of the property on various grounds. It may be argued that the respondent would incriminate himself (*British Phonographic Industry Ltd., sup. cit.,* and see discussion above); or that the communication is between law agent and client (*Micosta S.A.* v. *Shetland Islands Council,* 1983 S.L.T. 483); or that a communication is made for the purpose of litigation (*Young* v. *National Coal Board,* 1957 S.C. 99; *Johnstone* v. *National Coal Board,* 1968 S.C. 128; *Dobbie* v. *Forth Ports Authority,* 1974 S.C. 40; *Marks & Spencer* v. *British Gas Corp.,* 1983 S.L.T. 196; *More* v. *Brown & Root Wimpey Highland Fabricators,* 1983 S.L.T. 669; *Govan* v. *National Coal Board,* 1987 S.L.T. 511); or that the respondent has a lien (*Yau* v. *Ogilvie & Co.,* 1985 S.L.T. 91); or, generally, the document or property is not within the class which may be recovered (*Santa Fe International Corp.* v. *Napier Shipping S.A.,* 1985 S.L.T. 430). The Lord Advocate may argue that recovery is contrary to the public interest (*Friel* v. *Chief Constable of Strathclyde,* 1981 S.C. 1; *P. Cannon (Garages) Ltd.* v. *Lord Advocate,* 1983 S.L.T. (Sh.Ct.) 50).

5. Where the holder of documents claims confidentiality the items recovered are sealed. These documents cannot be opened or put in the process except by the authority of the court. This authority is obtained on a motion. Intimation of the motion should be made to the party, parties or third party have to give them an opportunity to be heard (rule 98).

Medical records

When it is necessary to recover medical records it will usually not be necessary to execute a commission. If the records are held by a state hospital intimation of the specification should be made to the Lord Advocate before the application for a commission and diligence is submitted to the court (*Glacken* v. *National Coal Board,* 1951 S.C. 82). A solicitor has a duty to provide a general medical practitioner or other medical attendant with a copy of the records (see *Practice Note,* December 14, 1972). Delays in the return of hospital records have caused problems (see *Practice Note,* September 15, 1983). Solicitors have a duty to return medical records to health boards as soon as it is known that the documents are no longer required or as soon as a cause is concluded. Records needed for treatment should be made available immediately on request from the hospital. Difficulties have also arisen from lack of care of hospital records (*Practice Note,* November 15, 1957).

CHAPTER 8

COMPANY PETITIONS

Introduction

It is not practicable within the compass of this book to give details of all the possible petitions which may be presented relating to companies. Separate chapters of this book deal with petitions which relate to an administration order (Chapter 2), liquidation (Chapter 16), and receivers (Chapter 19).

Company voluntary arrangements under Part 1 of the Insolvency Act 1986 are governed by rules 203 to 208 which were inserted by the Act of Sederunt (Rules of Court Amendment No. 11) (Companies) 1986 (S.I. 1986 No. 2298). This new procedure is intended to supplement the existing procedures for schemes of arrangement under sections 425–427 of the Companies Act 1985 which proved cumbersome to operate. The new procedure involves a relatively informal application to the insolvency judge by letter and report. If, for some reason, it is necessary to use the procedure by petition under the Companies Act, with its many hazards, the procedure will be found in D. Maxwell, *The Practice of the Court of Session*, p. 517.

Applications under the Company Directors Disqualification Act 1986 are made by petition presented in the Outer House and are dealt with by the insolvency judge (see rule 218N).

This chapter concentrates on what were, until August 3, 1987, the three most common Inner House petitions, namely petitions for confirmation of the reduction of capital, petitions for the rectification of the register of charges, and petitions for restoration to the register. Mention is also made of petitions for the protection of company members against unfair prejudice.

Outer House or Inner House?

The rules used to provide that, broadly speaking, all company petitions were Inner House petitions, except petitions relating to insolvency or similar proceedings. On occasion this caused confusion, particularly with petitions which sought more than one remedy. The position has been clarified since August 3, 1987 when there came into operation the Act of Sederunt (Rules of Court Amendment No. 4) (Miscellaneous) 1987 (S.I. 1987 No. 1206). Rules 189 (*a*) (v) and 190 (viii) are redefined with the effect that petitions under the Companies Acts or the Insolvency Act 1986 are Outer House petitions except petitions under sections 136 (reduction of capital) or 425 of the Companies Act 1985 (schemes of arrangement) which remain in the Inner House.

Jurisdiction

A reference to the "court" in the Companies Act 1985 usually means the court having jurisdiction to wind up the company (s. 744, 1985 Act). The winding-up jurisdiction of the court is governed by sections 120 and 221 of the Insolvency Act 1986.

In cases of judicial arrangements and similar proceedings the provisions of the Civil Jurisdiction and Judgments Act 1982 are excluded by the terms of article 1 of the 1968 Convention. Schedule 4 does not apply because of Schedule 5, para. 1 and Schedule 8 does not apply because of Schedule 9, para. 4. But the 1982 Act provides that certain courts have exclusive jurisdiction in relation to the validity of the constitution, the nullity or the dissolution of companies or, when the Convention applies, the decisions of companies' organs (see Sched. 1, art. 16 (2); Sched. 4, art. 16 (2); Sched. 8, art. 4 (1) (*b*)). The courts which have exclusive jurisdiction are those where the company has its "seat" (see A. E. Anton, *Civil Jurisdiction in Scotland* (1984), para. 4–22). Courts for the place where a register is kept also have exclusive jurisdiction in proceedings which have as their object the validity of entries in public registers (Sched. 1, art. 16 (3); Sched. 4, art. 16 (3)); Sched. 8, art. 4 (1) (*c*)). To add to the plethora of provisions Schedule 9 excludes from the Scottish rules (which are subject to the 1968 Convention and the inter-United Kingdom scheme) proceedings relating to a company where, by any enactment, jurisdiction in respect of those proceedings is conferred on the court having jurisdiction to wind it up.

The practical result is that in almost all cases of petitions to which this chapter relates the Court of Session will have jurisdiction if the company is registered in Scotland but exceptional and difficult cases may arise.

Reduction of capital

Petitions for confirmation of reduction of capital have been competent since the Companies Act 1867. The first petition presented was *Gartcraig Coal and Fire Co.* (1873) 10 S.L.R. 437. An early feature was a remit to a reporter. In 1928 the Second Division wrestled with the problem of whether a remit could be dispensed with. After first deciding that in one set of circumstances it could be, then reluctantly following that decision, it was finally decided to adopt the practice of remitting (*Fowlers*

(Aberdeen) Ltd., 1928 S.C. 186; *Scottish Stamping and Engineering Co.*, 1928 S.C. 484; *Hay & Sons*, 1928 S.C. 622). Another problem was settled over the years. Earlier provisions which resulted in the words "and reduced" being added to a company's name, at least for a limited period, were modified (Companies Act 1928, s. 19 (1); see now Companies Act 1985, s. 137 (2)) with the result that the words are added only if the court so orders (which it never does).

The procedure varies according to whether or not the court settles a list of creditors entitled to object to the petition in terms of section 136 (4). The petitioner will usually wish to avoid the trouble and expense of preparation of a list of the creditors of the company. The court may dispense with a list but only if a proposed reduction involves diminishing liability on unpaid capital or the payment to a shareholder of paid-up share capital (s. 136 (6)). There can be other reasons for the petition such as the cancellation of paid-up share capital (s. 135 (2)). A list of creditors can be dispensed with if the company holds sufficient cash and gilt-edged securities to cover all its proveable liabilities, as well as the amount, if any, which it is proposed to return to the shareholders (*Anderson Brown & Co. Ltd., Petrs.*, 1965 S.C. 81). The question is whether the interests of creditors are prejudiced and the assets of the company which are taken into account can include the debts due to the company (*Anderson Brown & Co. Ltd., sup. cit.*) including loans due from subsidiaries (*House of Fraser plc* v. *A.C.G.E. Investments Ltd.*, 1987 S.L.T. 273; 1987 S.L.T. 421). The normal procedure used to be to dispense with the settlement of the list of creditors *in hoc statu* before the remit to the reporter (*Clyde Structural Iron Co.*, 1930 S.C. 785) and, after considering the report, a direction would be made that the appropriate provisions of the Act did not apply to the creditors of the company or any class of them (*Unifruitco Steamship Co.*, 1930 S.C. 1104). As explained below, the present Second Division does not always follow this practice.

The procedure considered below is that of a simple petition for reduction of capital. For a petition which is combined with a scheme of arrangement see *Wilson Brothers and D. G. Howat & Co. Ltd.*, 1939 S.L.T. 68. The petition seeks confirmation of a reduction and it is worthwhile prior to the presentation of the petition to check whether the procedure to that date has been in order. As a minimum the following points should be looked at:

1. The company should be a company within the definitions of "company" and, where appropriate, "existing company" in section 735 of the Companies Act 1985. Occasionally someone

attempts to use the procedures of the Companies Acts for a company which was not registered under the Acts.

2. The Court of Session should have jurisdiction. See the definition of "court" in section 744 and the terms of section 120 of the Insolvency Act 1986. The court usually has jurisdiction because the company is registered in Scotland (see p. 52).

3. The articles of association (not the memorandum of association) must contain power to reduce capital (s. 135 (1)).

4. The company must have passed a valid resolution for reduction of its capital. Section 378 (2) states that a special resolution requires "not less than 21 days' notice." In *Neil McLeod & Sons Ltd., Petrs.*, 1967 S.C. 16 this was interpreted as not meaning 21 clear days. But it should be noted that the articles of the company may provide for 21 clear days. This will be the case if the company has adopted Table A, reg. 38 of the Companies (Table A to F) Regulations 1985 (S.I. 1985 No. 805). There is some doubt about whether the company must call a meeting, with notice, or whether it is sufficient to have a declaration signed by all the shareholders. In England it has been held that a meeting must be called (*Re Barry Artist Ltd.* [1985] 1 W.L.R. 1305). On omission to serve notice on all the members see *Re West Canadian Collieries* [1962] Ch. 370 and *Musselwhite* v. *C. H. Musselwhite & Son Ltd.* [1962] Ch. 964.

5. The meeting must have had a quorum. See *Neil McLeod & Sons Ltd., Petrs., sup. cit.* and M. C. Meston, 1967 S.L.T. (News) 117.

6. The procedure for the meeting laid down in the articles should have been followed and it is advisable to have the procedure minuted. Complications arising from a failure to follow the articles are illustrated by *The Citizens Theatre Ltd.*, 1946 S.C. 14 (articles required a "show of hands") and *Fraserburgh Commercial Co.*, 1946 S.C. 444 (minute failed to record a "show of hands").

7. It needs to be considered whether separate class meetings of members should have been held (*House of Fraser plc* v. *A.C.G.E. Investments Ltd.*, 1987 S.L.T. 421). The court has a duty to satisfy itself that the reduction is fair and equitable between the different classes of shareholders (*Wilsons and Clyde Coal Co.* v. *Scottish Insurance Corp.*, 1949 S.C. (H.L.) 90).

8. The special resolution must have been registered with the Registrar of Companies within 15 days in terms of section 380 (1) of the Companies Act 1985.

9. The draft minute in the petition should show the matters required by section 138 (1). The form of minute when an alteration

in capital structure was conditional on a reduction taking effect was discussed in *Doloi Tea Co. Ltd.,* 1961 S.L.T. 168.

10. If the company is a public company check if there are complications caused by a reduction of the capital below the authorised minimum (see s. 139).

No procedure applies to all circumstances but the steps commonly taken in the petition are:

1. Ten prints of the petition are lodged, a process and an inventory of productions with various productions which may include:

(a) a copy of the company's memorandum and articles of association. This should be an up-to-date version. Note that the issue of a memorandum which does not embody registered alterations is an offence (Companies Act 1985, s. 20);

(b) a certified copy of the notice calling the meeting to consider the special resolution;

(c) certificates of posting of notices (or other evidence that notice was given to, or dispensed with by, shareholders);

(d) certified copy of the minutes of the meeting;

(e) registrar of companies' receipt for lodging a copy of the special resolution;

(f) certified copy of the latest annual report and accounts.

2. The petition seeks *inter alia* an order for intimation on the walls and in the minute book, and advertisement in the *Edinburgh Gazette* and newspapers. Without a motion being enrolled an interlocutor should be passed which orders intimation and advertisement. Normally no service is required because the petitioner is the company.

3. An execution copy petition is lodged accompanied by an inventory of productions and copies of the *Gazette* and newspapers containing advertisements. A motion is enrolled, "To remit the petition to a reporter and to dispense *in hoc statu* with the provisions of section 136 (3) to (5) of the Companies Act 1985." This will be a starred motion. In recent practice, however, the Second Division has refused to dispense *in hoc statu* with the provisions of sections 136 (3) to (5) on the grounds that this is unnecessary. When the motion for a remit is granted, the petitioner's solicitor will obtain a certified copy of the interlocutor, borrow the execution copy petition and productions and send the papers to the reporter.

4. The reporter's report is lodged. It is treated like a principal writ and so 10 copies should be lodged (see rule 26). It will be necessary also, if not done earlier, to lodge four copies of the

productions for use by the court. A motion is enrolled, "On behalf of the petitioner to approve the report No. — of process, to dispense with the provisions of section 136 (3) to (5) of the Companies Act 1985 and in respect that the court has jurisdiction as averred in paragraph X of the petition to grant the prayer of the petition." This will be a starred motion. It is the duty of the court to consider the interests of creditors, shareholders and the public (*Westburn Sugar Refineries Ltd.*, 1951 S.C. (H.L.) 57).

5. If the motion is granted the interlocutor dispenses with the requirements of section 136 (3) to (5), confirms the reduction of capital, approves the proposed minute, directs registration of the court order and the minute with the registrar of companies and then advertisement in the *Gazette* and a newspaper or newpapers. This extra advertisement may seem an unnecessary expense but section 138 (3) provides that registration shall be published in such manner as the court may direct.

6. A certified copy interlocutor is obtained which incorporates a certified copy of the minute. Intimation is made to the registrar and thereafter advertisement as directed.

7. The reduction does not take effect until the order and minute are registered (s. 138 (2)). A petition to the *nobile officium* when shareholders were paid out prior to the presentation of the petition was refused in *Alex Henderson Ltd., Petrs.*, 1967 S.L.T. (Notes) 17. After registration the company may make payments to shareholders or issue new share certificates as apppropriate.

8. The minute, when registered, is deemed to be an alteration of the memorandum (s. 138 (5) and (6)).

If it is necessary to settle a list of creditors, the list should contain a statement of the name and address of each creditor, the amount of the debt and the nature of the debt (see s. 136 (3)). A motion would be enrolled to fix a date with reference to which the list of creditors shall be made up and to appoint the company to lodge the list in process. The list would be lodged and a second motion enrolled to fix a date on or before which the creditors not entered on the list are to claim to be so entered or are to be excluded from the right to object to the reduction of capital. The interlocutor which fixes that second date would require advertisement in the *Edinburgh Gazette* and in newspapers. The *Gazette* and newspapers would be lodged in process with an inventory and a motion enrolled to settle the list and for an order for creditors to lodge answers or consents to the petition.

There would be intimation of a copy of the petition by registered or recorded delivery to each creditor whose name is entered on the list. The intimation should contain a copy of the petition and of the list (or at least, of the particulars in the list which relate to the person to whom intimation is made), and a copy of the court interlocutor. Evidence of the intimation should be lodged in process.

If answers or objections are lodged by any creditor the court would require to dispose of the matter by a hearing. The court can dispense with the consent of a creditor to the reduction if payment of the debt is secured (s. 136 (5)). If no answers or objections are lodged a motion should be enrolled to find that the creditors have consented to the reduction (and that debts have been discharged or determined or secured, as appropriate. See s. 136 (5)). It may also be appropriate at this point to seek approval of the reporter's report and for the prayer of the petition to be granted.

Rectification of register of charges

In terms of section 410 of the Companies Act 1958 every charge created by a company, and to which the section applies, must be registered with the registrar of companies within 21 days after the date of creation of the charge. The section applies to the charges listed in section 410 (4) which refers to many (but not all) of the fixed securities which might be created by a company and also mentions a floating charge. Under section 419 a memorandum of satisfaction may be registered.

Section 420 provides:

> "The court, on being satisfied that the omission to register a charge within the time required by this Act or that the omission or mis-statement of any particular with respect to any such charge or in a memorandum of satisfaction was accidental, or due to inadvertence or to some other sufficient cause, or is not of a nature to prejudice the position of creditors or shareholders of the company, or that it is on other grounds just and equitable to grant relief, may, on the application of the company or any person interested, and on such terms and conditions as seem to the court just and expedient, order that the time for registration shall be extended or (as the case may be) that the omission or mis-statement shall be rectified."

A petition under the section is now an Outer House petition (see p. 51). The procedure in the typical petition is as follows:

1. The petition is lodged with a process, a copy of the petition for the Advocates' Library and an inventory of productions with productions such as a copy of a standard security. The petition

may be either by the creditor or by the company or any person interested. The petition seeks service on the Lord Advocate, and on either the company or the creditor, as appropriate.

2. There is the usual order for intimation and service without the enrolment of a motion. After intimation and service an execution copy petition is lodged and a motion is enrolled to grant the prayer of the petition. The motion will be starred.

3. After hearing the motion the court may pronounce an interlocutor which extends the time for registration of the charge by a period which varies from seven to 21 days or the interlocutor, if appropriate, may rectify an omission or misstatement.

4. The petitioner's solicitor obtains a certified copy of the interlocutor for exhibition to the Registrar of Companies and the solicitor registers the charge within the period allowed or otherwise gives effect to the interlocutor.

Restoration to the register

In the typical case the petition arises because the Registrar of Companies has struck the company off the register in terms of section 652 of the Companies Act 1985. The Registrar carries out the procedure in section 652, usually because the company has failed to lodge annual returns. On the publication of a second *Gazette* notice the company is dissolved (s. 652 (5)). At some stage those responsible for the company's affairs discover what has happened. There is distress because the property of the company has become *bona vacantia* and belongs to the Crown (s. 654). A petition to restore the company to the register is presented in terms of section 653. A petition under the section is now an Outer House petition (see p. 51).

1. The petition is lodged with a process, a copy of the petition for the Advocates' Library and an inventory of productions and productions. The petitioner can be the company, a member or a creditor (s. 653 (2)). The petition can be presented within 20 years of the *Gazette* notice (s. 653 (2)).

2. The prayer of the petition will seek intimation on the walls and in the minute book and service. Service should be sought on the Registrar of Companies and the Lord Advocate. Normally there will also be advertisement in the *Edinburgh Gazette*. The usual *induciae* for answers will be 21 days. Sometimes an attempt is made to shorten this. This must be done by motion (rule 192 (3)) and it would be a starred motion. An interlocutor is granted ordering intimation, service and advertisement.

3. After compliance with the first interlocutor an execution copy petition is lodged with, if appropriate, an inventory of productions

with *Gazette* and newspapers. A motion is enrolled to grant the prayer of the petition.

4. The court may grant an interlocutor in the following form:

"The Lord Ordinary having considered the petition and proceedings, no answers having been lodged, orders that the name of X limited be restored to the Register of Companies; directs the Registrar of Companies to advertise this order in his official name in the *Edinburgh Gazette*; authorises the expenses of this application and of the procedure following thereon including the expenses to be paid to the said registrar to be paid out of the first and readiest funds of the company and decerns."

5. The solicitor for the petitioner obtains a certified copy of the interlocutor. On its delivery to the Registrar of Companies the company is deemed to have continued in existence as if its name had not been struck off (s. 653 (3)).

Unfair prejudice

A petition may be presented under section 459 of the Companies Act 1985 for protection of a company's members against unfair prejudice. This section has antecedents in section 75 of the Companies Act 1980 and section 210 of the Companies Act 1948. A petition under the section is now an Outer House petition (see p. 51). The petition is sometimes combined with a request to wind up the company on the grounds that it is just and equitable to do so (Insolvency Act 1986, s. 122 (1) (*g*); see *Ebrahimi* v. *Westbourne Galleries Ltd.* [1973] A.C. 360); *Gammack* v. *Mitchells (Fraserburgh) Ltd.*, 1983 S.C. 39).

On a motion being enrolled the court may make an interim order such as an order which prevents a meeting being held or a director being dismissed (*Whyte, Petr.*, 1984 S.L.T. 330) or allotment of shares and disposal of property (*Malaga Investments Ltd., Petrs.*, 1987 G.W.D. 20–757). A motion may be enrolled to appoint a judicial factor *ad interim* (see p. 89).

A *caveat* may be lodged against a section 459 petition (see p. 6).

The terms of section 461 allow the court to make such order as it thinks fit for giving relief in respect of the matters complained of. The prayer of the petition should, however, narrate the order which the petitioner seeks. The various types of orders which might be sought are discussed in D. P. Sellar, "Section 75 of the Companies Act 1980," 1984 S.L.T. (News) 310 and 317; *Re Bird*

Precision Bellows Ltd. [1986] 2 W.L.R. 158; *Re a Company* [1986] 2 All E.R. 253; *Re London School of Electronics Ltd* [1986] Ch. 211; *cf. Re a Company* [1987] 1 W.L.R. 102.

The petition is always by a member or a person to whom shares have transmitted by operation of law (s. 459).

Because of the possibility of interim orders and the variety of other orders which might be sought it is more than usually difficult to provide a model procedure. What might happen is this:

1. The petition is lodged with a process, a copy of the petition for the Advocates' Library and an inventory of productions and productions. There is the usual first order for intimation and service.

2. An execution copy petition will be lodged. It would be common for answers to be lodged within the induciae. A motion would be enrolled to allow the petition and answers to be adjusted. This motion may be enrolled by either party. The authority of the court is needed for adjustment (rule 196 (*c*)). After adjustment there may be a motion to print a record. An interlocutor may give authority to print a record and appoint a hearing or a proof. Further procedure, whether by way of a hearing or a proof or proof before answer, depends on the nature of the dispute. The dispute might be settled and the final disposal could arise on authority being interponed to a joint minute. If a proof was necessary a motion may be enrolled. "On behalf of the petitioner for authority to print a record on the petition and answers as adjusted, and to allow a proof on the petition and answers as adjusted." This would be an unstarred motion.

3. An interim order may be sought by motion at any time and could be granted with the interlocutor for intimation and service.

CHAPTER 9

CURATOR BONIS

Preliminary matters

Prior to the presentation of a petition for the appointment of a *curator bonis* the petitioner's solicitor should be satisfied on the following points.

1. The Court of Session must have jurisdiction. It is relevant to consider whether the *incapax* is domiciled or resident or possessed of property in Scotland (J. C. Irons, *Judicial Factors* (1908), p. 298; J. A. Maclaren, *Bill Chamber Practice* (1915), p. 126). Mere ownership of moveables in Scotland by a foreign *incapax* may not justify appointment. As Professor Anton puts it:

> "No Scottish case has been traced in which the grounds of jurisdiction to appoint curators are comprehensively examined. In several of the reported cases no opinions were given and it is not always easy to see whether a particular decision was based upon general principles or upon the particular facts of the case. It seems clear, however, that jurisdiction cannot turn exclusively either upon the local situation of the *incapax* himself or upon that of his property. It is necessary to protect, or to attempt to protect, both the foreign property of a Scottish *incapax* and the Scottish property of a foreign *incapax*. No tidy general rule, then, is likely to be established and the cases suggest that such rules as have been evolved should be stated as directing principles rather than hard and fast rules. The dominant theme is the protection of the *incapax* and the court will always make an appointment which is required either by the urgency of the situation or by the special facts of the case." (*Private International Law* (1967), pp. 380, 381.)

If a *curator bonis* is appointed under Scots law for any person suffering from mental disorder the provisions of Scots law apply in relation to the property (other than land) and affairs of that person in Northern Ireland unless a committee, receiver or guardian has been appointed in Northern Ireland (Mental Health (Scotland) Act 1984, s. 95 (1)). Similar reciprocal arrangements exist with England and Wales (Mental Health Act 1983, s. 110). A certified copy interlocutor of the appointment of a curator has effect throughout the British Dominions (Judicial Factors (Scotland) Act

1889, s. 13, as amended by Act of Sederunt of March 17, 1967 and see discussion at p. 67).

As a question of the capacity of a natural person is in issue the jurisdiction rules of the Civil Jurisdiction and Judgments Act 1982 are inapplicable (see Sched. 1, art. 1; Sched. 9, para. 3). Section 16 of the Family Law Act 1986 does not apply to the appointment or removal of a *curator bonis* (or factor *loco tutoris*) or any application made by a *curator bonis* or factor *loco tutoris* (s. 16 (2)). But section 16 does regulate the jurisdiction of the court in the appointment of any other form of curator or tutor.

2. Grounds for appointment must exist. The usual (if not the invariable) ground for appointment is that a person "is of unsound mind and incapable of managing his affairs or giving instructions for their management." It will be noticed that this states three things. A person could be psychotic but still capable of dealing with his property without detriment to himself or a person could be paralysed but still capable of giving instructions. (See N. M. L. Walker, *Judicial Factors* (1974), pp. 22–24.)

3. Two medical certificates in the appropriate form must be lodged with the petition. The certificates no longer need to be on soul and conscience (*Practice Note*, June 6, 1968). Each certificate should be holograph of, or adopted as holograph by, the doctor. A certificate should design the doctor and state when and where the *incapax* was examined. The examination should be within 30 days prior to the presentation of the petition in the normal case. It was stated by Sheriff N. M. L. Walker that if the *incapax* was an inmate of an asylum, one of the certificates must be by a doctor who was not connected with the institution (*op. cit.*, p. 24). This rule is no longer followed in practice. With the introduction of the National Health Service it is less likely than it was formerly that the hospital would benefit from keeping the patient. If the *incapax* has been in hospital for some time it may not be practicable to obtain an up-to-date assessment from the patient's general practitioner. The hospital doctors may be the best qualified to issue the certificates. It is common to have both certificates granted by doctors who work in the same hospital.

Antonio stated that each medical man should make his examination outwith the presence of the other, although it is not necessary to state the fact in the certificates (D. Antonio, *Forms and Precedents in the Bill Chamber* (1905), p. 138). It is not the practice to inquire about this. If there is a contested petition and a conflict of view on the health of the *incapax*, the likely course is a remit by the court to a neutral doctor who is specially qualified in the treatment of mental disorders (*Brown* v. *Hackston*, 1960

S.C. 27; *Fraser* v. *Paterson*, 1987 S.L.T. 562; sequel 1987 S.C.L.R. 577.

If service of the petition on the *incapax* is to be dispensed with, the medical certificates should state that it would be harmful to the health of the *incapax* if service were to be made upon him (rule 191 (*c*)). If special powers to sell the *incapax's* house are to be sought by the curator following his appointment the medical certificates should state that the *incapax* will never return to the house or otherwise indicate the doctors' views.

4. There must be an appropriate petitioner. A wide range of persons may petition (see Walker, *op. cit.*, p. 25). The usual petitioner is a relative. The Mental Welfare Commission may petition (Mental Health (Scotland) Act 1984, s. 93).

5. The proper respondents to the petition are all those, other than the petitioner, who are interested in the estate of the *incapax*. These will normally be the *incapax* and his near relatives. It should be checked that the names and designations of those mentioned in the schedule for service correspond to the details given in the body of the petition.

6. The proposed curator must not have an interest which is adverse to that of the *incapax*. If the proposed curator is not resident in Scotland it is necessary for him to sign a bond of prorogation and a style of this bond is in Chapter 26. In the normal case only one person will be appointed as *curator bonis*. Appointments of more than one person to the same office are exceptional (J. C. Irons, *Judicial Factors*, (1908) pp. 32 and 274). The complication which arises if the proposed curator is not a professional nominee is mentioned later. The curator must be an individual and cannot be a limited company (*Brogan, Petr.*, 1986 S.L.T. 420).

7. An inventory of the *incapax's* estate must be prepared. The value of the estate will affect the amount of caution to be fixed by the Accountant of Court.

Procedure

The procedure followed in the normal case is:

1. A petition is lodged with a process, a copy of the petition for the Advocates' Library, a copy of the petition for the Accountant of Court (rule 200 (*a*)), and an inventory of productions with the two medical certificates. If a bond of prorogation is needed it should be lodged at any time up to the lodging of the bond of caution. Failure to lodge the bond of prorogation in time will result in the Accountant of Court retaining the process and while

the process is in his possession it will not be possible to obtain a certified copy interlocutor of the curator's appointment.

2. There will be an interlocutor for intimation and service without enrolling a motion (rule 195) except in two circumstances. First, if the prayer of the petition seeks to dispense with service on the *incapax*, a motion must be enrolled to dispense with this service. Secondly, if the petition seeks the appointment of a curator who is not a professional nominee, a motion must be enrolled for intimation and service. The question of an appointment and further procedure will be decided by a Lord Ordinary.

3. If it is desired to appoint an interim curator a motion for this must be enrolled. There should be suitable averments in the petition to justify an interim appointment. The motion will be starred. The style of interlocutor indicates what should happen following the appointment. The interlocutor will be in approximately these terms:

> "Meantime pending the currency of the intimation and service and until the petition for a permanent appointment has been granted or refused Nominates and Appoints A [design] to be *curator bonis ad interim* to B designed in the petition with the usual powers and authorises the said A after finding caution to enter upon the duties of his office upon a certified copy of this interlocutor with a schedule of the curatory estate annexed thereto and Appoints the interim curator to communicate with the Accountant of Court at intervals of not more than one month until the appointment has been made permanent."

The one-month rule is based on *McCulloch* v. *McCulloch*, 1953 S.C. 189. This case states also that an interim appointment has effect notwithstanding a reclaiming motion.

4. Intimation and service is carried out in the normal way with this speciality. Service on the *incapax*, if it is to take place, is almost always personal service. Where personal service was prohibitively expensive the court authorised postal service (*Robertson, Petr.*, 1978 S.L.T. (Notes) 39).

5. After the expiry of the *induciae* an execution copy petition is lodged in process and a motion enrolled to grant the prayer of the petition and for expenses. This form of motion is inappropriate if the prayer of the petition seeks special powers, such as authority to sell heritage. The reason is that normally the appropriate applicant for the powers is the curator who should be appointed before the powers are sought. Irons mentions a power to make up titles as being the only special power ever granted at the time of

appointment (J. C. Irons, *Judicial Factors* (1908), p. 319). There is old authority for this limited exception where the estimate is small (*Brodie* (1867) 3 S.L.R. 223). In a more recent reported case Lord Cameron granted special powers at the same time as appointing the curator, but the case has the speciality that the petitioner sought his own appointment as curator (*Barclay, Petr.*, 1962 S.C. 594). The normal procedure if special powers are sought is that the motion at this stage is for the appointment of the curator. Expenses are not sought until after the prayer of the petition is exhausted.

6. Normally all motions which involve the appointment of a curator will be unstarred. The interlocutor (where special powers are not sought) will narrate that the court:

> "no Answers having been lodged, Nominates and Appoints A [design] to be *curator bonis* to B designed in the Petition with the usual powers and decerns; authorises the said A after finding caution to enter on the duties of his office upon a certified copy of this interlocutor with a schedule of the curatory estate annexed thereto: finds the petitioner entitled to the expenses of this application and procedure following thereon out of the curatory estate, and remits the account thereof, when lodged, to the Auditor of Court for taxation."

7. The time for finding caution is limited to one calendar month from the date of the interlocutor which appoints the curator. A motion may be enrolled *before* the expiry of this period to prorogate the time for finding caution (rule 200 (*c*)). This is giving rise to some problems because the office of the Accountant of Court has moved to Meldrum House. He may have possession of the process and it may be necessary either to arrange for retransmission of the process to the petition department or for the petitioner's solicitor to enrol the motion at Meldrum House with a request for retransmission. If enrolment of the motion for prorogation is left to the last minute (and it usually is) the petitioner's solicitor should be aware that practical difficulties may arise because of the whereabouts of the motion sheet. If the one-month period expires without caution being found or the time prorogated, the appointment of the curator falls (Judicial Factors Act 1849, s. 2). A motion for a new appointment should then be enrolled. The court will normally direct that the expenses of this motion should not be charged against the curatory estate.

8. The new insolvency procedures which dispense with the lodging of a bond of caution in process do not apply to curatories. The procedure in finding caution in a curatory is regulated by rule

200 (*e*). The process is transmitted by the petition department to the Accountant of Court. On receipt of the process the Accountant issues caution forms in duplicate which ask for details of the appointment and the value of the estate. Frequently these are returned marked "as in petition." It is possible that in the near future the procedure will be changed and in the vast majority of cases caution will be fixed by reference to the details in the petition without the necessity for the completion of caution forms. The caution is based on the value of the estate with the minimum being two-thirds of the value of the moveable and other readily realisable assets (rule 200 (*e*) (ii). The Accountant never fixes caution at less than the sum covered by the minimum premium. That sum, at the moment, is £20,000. The Accountant checks that the solicitor's values are realistic and takes account of current income. If the curatory petition has a prayer for special powers and it is likely that heritage will be sold within 12 months, the potential sale proceeds are relevant. One completed caution form is retained by the Accountant and the other is sent to the solicitor.

Once a bond of caution for the appropriate amount has been delivered to the Accountant he marks on the interlocutor sheet that caution has been found and the process is returned to the petition department. Only once this has been done can a certified copy of the interlocutor which appointed the curator be issued (Judicial Factors Act 1849, s. 2, as amended).

Within six months from the date on which the bond of caution is delivered the curator must lodge with the Accountant an inventory of the estate (Judicial Factors Act 1849, s. 3 and see "Notes for the Guidance of Judicial Factors" printed in the *Parliament House Book)*. This inventory may disclose an alteration in the estate. There may also be additional estate specially reported to the Accountant. The result may be a need to alter the amount of caution. This is done by a memorandum of agreement, not by a new bond. The curator obtains the memorandum from the insurance company. The Accountant used to obtain the process from the petition department and mark the alteration of the amount of caution in the margin of the interlocutor sheet. This procedure has been dispensed with by agreement with the Lord President. The court is interested only in the fact that caution has been obtained: the amount of the caution is a matter for the Accountant.

9. The curator has a statutory duty to obtain a certified copy interlocutor of his appointment without delay (Judicial Factors Act 1849, s. 2). The petition department prepare certified copy interlocutors of a curator's appointment, contrary to the normal

rule that certified copy interlocutors are prepared by the solicitor and certified by the court staff. The schedule to the interlocutor will include moveable estate only. It is not essential that all items of the ward's estate appear in the schedule. Section 13 of the Judicial Factors (Scotland) Act 1889 as amended by Act of Sederunt of March 17, 1967, gives to the certified copy inter-locutor the effect of a transfer to the curator of all the property of the ward in the British Dominions. At one time, when extract decrees were issued of appointments, it was rare to append a note of the estate. A problem arose with the Bank of England as result of which section 66 of the Finance Act 1916 was passed. This makes the interlocutor sufficient to transfer government stock if the stock is specified in the appendix to the interlocutor or is certified by the Accountant of Court as forming part of the ward's estate. Presumably to avoid the need for certification the practice evolved of specifying the moveable estate in the interlocutor and that practice has become standard. It remains the case, however, that by statute the curator's appointment is his authority to deal with the ward's estate and that is not removed by errors in the specification of the estate which may have been made when his appointment was sought.

In practice there are few calls on the Accountant for certifi-cation. If the ward has estate in a foreign country the appropriate foreign embassy in Britain is approached and on their certification of a copy of the interlocutor it is almost invariably possible to obtain remittance of funds. If the ward has heritage in England, the curator applies to the Court of Session for power to sell and then, if appropriate, makes application to an English court. In practice sometimes the authority of an English court is obtained and sometimes it is not.

10. To minimise expense special powers may be craved in the petition for appointment. Although the petition applies for special powers the court does not grant powers to the petitioner but to the curator. The curator may enrol a motion for a remit to the Accountant of Court to report on the special powers (see Judicial Factors Act 1849, s. 7). On the interlocutor being granted the process is remitted to the Accountant by the petition department. The Accountant reports in writing. The report and, if appropriate, an inventory of productions with any relevant papers (*e.g.* a surveyor's valuation of heritage) are lodged in process. A motion is enrolled, "On behalf of the *curator bonis*, in respect of the re-port by the Accountant of Court number — of process, to grant the special powers craved in the petition and for expenses." This is an appropriate motion even if the Accountant's report is unfavourable.

There has to be an interlocutor on the special powers to exhaust the prayer of the petition before the petitioner can obtain an award of expenses. The solicitor has a duty to supply to the Accountant copies of interlocutors which grant or refuse special powers within two days of issue (rule 200 (*a*)).

The petition department do not prepare certified copy interlocutors which grant special powers. The clerks may advise that if a link in title is sought, an extract decree might be more acceptable.

Special powers

A curator may seek special powers either (a) in the prayer of the petition for appointment (see above) or (b) by application to the court by note (p. 70) or (c) by application to the Accountant of Court under the Trusts (Scotland) Act 1961, s. 2 (3) to (6) as those subsections were added by the Law Reform (Miscellaneous Provisions) (Scotland) Act 1980, s. 8 (p. 70) or (d) by petition for authority under section 5 of the Trusts (Scotland) Act 1921 (p. 151). In matters not covered by statutory provisions it may be possible to petition at common law (*Tennent's Judicial Factor* v. *Tennent*, 1954 S.C. 215) but such petitions are very uncommon.

The need for special powers

A curator's duty is to preserve the estate of the ward pending the recovery or death of the ward. In *Macqueen* v. *Tod* (1899) 1 F. 1069, at p. 1075 Lord President Robertson observed:

> "The most general of the principles of the law of guardianship is that the curator of an insane person is there to preserve the estate. He is to do so in the spirit of one whose ward may at any time come back to her full legal rights. He is therefore to keep things going, rather than to change; he is to do nothing that is irretrievable, unless in case of necessity; and he is to preserve, as far as possible, such options as are open in the management of the estate, reserving them for his ward if she convalesce, or, if not, then for her heirs. Moreover, one of his specific duties is not, by any voluntary act, to change the succession of the ward. With reference to one of the specialities of this case, I should say that the policy of the guardian will be especially conservative where the ward is of great age."

In that case the curator of a ward who was aged 85 presented a note to the court for authority to sell part of the trees on the ward's estate. The trees had reached maturity. The court refused authority and held that it was the duty of the curator to preserve the estate. One of the specialities which might have been referred to by Lord President Robertson was that the ward was an heiress of entail and on her death the heritable estate and the moveable estate had different destinations. There was in that case no need to produce funds for the maintenance of the ward. Although the interests of the estate and those who may succeed to it are important, the primary concern of the court is the interest of the ward (see at p. 1078 *per* Lord McLaren). It may be necessary to convert heritable estate into moveable if the ward can be maintained only by selling or burdening the heritable estate. A common circumstance which leads to an application for special powers is the need to sell the ward's dwelling-house so that funds may be released to pay for the maintenance of the ward in a nursing home. But the frequency of this type of application tends to obscure in the mind of practitioners the general principle that the curator's duty is to preserve the estate. A curator need not attempt to improve or increase the estate (*Burns' Curator Bonis* v. *Burns' Trs.*, 1961 S.L.T. 166 at p. 167 *per* Lord Kilbrandon). The court may order the curator to retain property and not dispose of it except with the leave of the court (*Browning's J. F.* (1905) 7 F. 1037; *Fraser* v. *Paterson*, 1987 S.L.T. 562; sequel 1987 S.C.L.R. 577).

Distinction between a curator and other factors or a trustee

A curator has certain powers under the Trusts (Scotland) Act 1921 and the Trustee Investments Act 1961. It does not follow that because a curator has powers the curator has a duty to exercise those powers. Indeed it may be quite wrong to do so. The powers under section 4 of the 1921 Act can be exercised only where the Act is "not at variance with the terms or purposes of the trust." Court authority under section 5 of the Act can be given only when the act "is in all the circumstances expedient." A curator is a form of judicial factor but factors are appointed for many different reasons and the exercise of powers will depend on the purposes of the appointment. The duty of some factors is to distribute an estate (see, for example, a factor on the estate of a deceased person at p. 89). A *curator bonis*, in contrast, has a duty to preserve the estate. A curator does not act like a trustee and the ward is not merely a beneficiary (*Inland Revenue* v. *McMillan's Curator Bonis*, 1956 S.C. 142). It follows that a curator may retain shares in a private company which are not authorised investments under the Trustee Investments Act 1961 (*Fraser, Petr.*, 1987 S.C.L.R. 577).

Application to the Accountant of Court for consent

Where a curator thinks it expedient to do an act of the type mentioned in section 4 (1) (*a*) to (*ee*) of the Trusts (Scotland) Act 1921 he may apply to the Accountant of Court for consent (Trusts (Scotland) Act 1961, s. 3 (3)). The procedure is governed by rule 200A.

A curator sends a letter to the Accountant and states what powers are requested and why they are necessary. On the date of this application or as soon as possible thereafter the curator sends a notice by recorded delivery post to the persons listed in rule 200A (2) and sends an execution of service to the Accountant. The notice must have the particulars specified in rule 200A (1). There is a 28-day period for objections to be sent by recorded delivery post to the Accountant and the curator. If there are no objections the Accountant may grant his consent if the conditions of section 2 (4) of the Trust (Scotland) Act 1961 are satisfied. The Accountant issues the appropriate document under his seal. If there are objections the Accountant will insist that a note for special powers is lodged in court under section 7 of the Judicial Factors Act 1849.

Note for special powers

A *curator bonis* may apply to the court under section 7 of the Judicial Factors Act 1849 for special powers. In the first instance the curator reports to the Accountant of Court. The curator should state the circumstances in a similar way to the averments in a petition. The report should conclude, as in the prayer of a petition, with a statement of the exact powers which the curator wishes from the court. The "Notes for the Guidance of Judicial Factors" state (para. 25 (a):

> "If the sale involves the ward's dwelling house or a property which is liferented by the ward, the Accountant requires a formal professional valuation of the subjects, along with evidence—normally an up-to-date medical report—that the ward's recovery is improbable or that, in any event, it is considered inadvisable he (or she) should resume occupation of the house or property. In all circumstances the factor must in addition satisfy the Accountant as to the terms and conditions of any sale he would propose to effect. No voluntary action by a factor can alter the succession to his ward's estate. Therefore the net proceeds of a sale remain and must be noted in the factor's accounts as heritable."

The Accountant of Court prepares his own report on the matter and sends it back to the curator or his solicitors for revisal. The final report by the Accountant and the curator's report eventually reach the curator's solicitors who are then able to instruct counsel to prepare the note.

As a general rule the court will only grant power to do a particular act (*e.g.* to sell X dwelling-house). It is exceptional for the court to grant power to do acts of a particular kind (*e.g.* to sell heritage). *Carmichaels J. F.* v. *Accountant of Court*, 1971 S.C. 295, is an example of powers craved being too wide and unspecific. On the incompetence of a third party claiming against the curator by note in the petition process see *Latta, Noter*, 1977 S.L.T. 127, and authorities there reviewed.

After the Accountant has prepared his report the procedure followed is:

1. A note is lodged in the original curatory process with a certified copy note and an inventory of productions with productions which may include the curator's report, the Accountant's report, a surveyor's report, and one medical certificate. A copy of the note for the Advocates' Library and for the Accountant are "boxed" (rule 200 (*a*)). The petition department staff will check that there are no obvious defects in the note such as a different designation of the curator from the interlocutor which appointed him. The practice where a medical certificate is required is to accept a certificate based on one examination within, approximately, the previous six months. The note is never served on the *incapax (Cameron's C.B.,* 1961 S.L.T. (Notes) 21).

2. There will be an order for intimation and service without a motion being enrolled. Service should be on the previous petitioner and all parties who were served in the petition for appointment (other than the *incapax*) and also on the cautioners.

3. After intimation and service an execution copy note will be lodged in process. A motion is enrolled to grant the prayer of the petition and for expenses. The motion will normally be unstarred. There is a special point on expenses if the curator is an Edinburgh solicitor. His firm is not allowed to charge professional fees to be paid out of the curatory estate. The reason is the principle which limits the extent to which a trustee can make a profit from his own office. Although much regretted by some judges the basis of the present rule was laid down in *Lord Gray* (1856) 19 D. 1, and confirmed in *Mitchell* v. *Burness* (1878) 5 R. 1124. The curator will be paid factorial commission fixed by the Accountant. This is based on a percentage of cash transactions and realisations and generally on the difficulty of managing the estate. Where the curator is a solicitor outside Edinburgh, and not practising in the Court of Session, his Edinburgh correspondent's fees will form a valid charge against the curatory estate. Problems have arisen in

recent years with Glasgow firms who have opened a branch office in Edinburgh. The curator may be based in Glasgow but it is his firm who present the note to the court and so the professional fees of the firm in the presentation of the note cannot be charged.

4. If the note is opposed and answers are lodged, there may be a remit to the Accountant to report, rather than a proof (*McInroy's C.B.* v. *McInroy*, 1966 S.L.T. (Notes) 72, following *Gilligan's Factor* v. *Fraser* (1898) 25 R. 876).

5. The court may refuse the special powers as unnecessary. This happens in practice in a very small percentage of cases. In these instances, nevertheless, the noter usually obtains an award of expenses. An instance of an application for power to buy heritage which was found justified but dismissed as unnecessary is *Bristow, Petr.*, 1965 S.L.T. 225. Where an interlocutor is granted which awards or refuses special powers it must be intimated within two days to the Accountant by the noter's solicitor (rule 200 (*a*)).

6. The interlocutor which grants authority to sell heritage will grant authority to sell in such manner and at such price as may be approved by the Accountant of Court. The petition department do not prepare certified copies of interlocutors which grant special powers. They may advise that if a link in title is needed, an extract decree might be more acceptable.

Petition for the exoneration and discharge of a curator, the incapax having died

It is for the curator to decide if he wishes a judicial discharge. The Accountant does not require it. An informal method of writing off a curatory and avoiding a formal discharge has been in operation for many years. This has the advantage of relative lack of expense compared with formal proceedings and at the same time it enables the court staff to treat the curatory as being finished. The curator either intimates his intention not to apply for a discharge or after a considerable period of time the curator fails to take steps to apply for a discharge. The Accountant prepares a short report. The Accountant sends this report to the petition department with a letter which makes an application to the court. If everything is in order a docquet is put on this report and signed by a judge "Duly noted." The bond of caution is not delivered.

The procedure for a formal discharge is as follows:

1. A petition and certified copy petition are lodged in the original curatory process. Copies are also boxed for the Advocates' Library and the Accountant of Court. There may be an inventory of productions with productions such as a death certificate or confirmation of executors. It is unnecessary to lodge

a certified copy of the interlocutor which appointed the curator because the petition is lodged in the original process. Service should be sought on relatives who have an interest, the curator's cautioners, and the *incapax's* executors.

2. Without enrolling a motion there will be an order for intimation and service. After these have been carried out an execution copy petition is lodged and a motion enrolled, "On behalf of the petitioner to remit to the Accountant of Court to report on the petitioner's intromissions with the estate with a view to his discharge (and for expenses)."

An interlocutor remits to the Accountant to report, finds the petitioner entitled to his expenses out of the estate and remits the account when lodged to the Auditor of Court for taxation. The petition department transmits the process to the Accountant. The *curator bonis* will lodge a final account of charge and discharge with the Accountant. The account of charge and discharge will contain the curator's intromissions to the date of death of the *incapax*. The solicitor's account of expenses is lodged in process and transmitted to the Accountant of Court for perusal before taxation by the Auditor of Court. This account forms no part of the final account of charge and discharge and the taxed account (which relates to a period after the death of the *incapax*) should be presented to the deceased *incapax's* executor for settlement. The Accountant requires to see the confirmation of executors and a receipt by the executors which acknowledges that the funds detailed in the receipt, the effects under the curatory and the title deeds of heritage have been handed over (see "Notes for Guidance of Judicial Factors"). The Accountant prepares his report, a draft being sent to the solicitor for his observations. When the final report is signed the process is retransmitted to the petition department.

3. A motion is enrolled, "On behalf of the petitioner in respect of the report of the Accountant of Court number — of process, for exoneration and discharge." An interlocutor is passed which discharges the curator and authorises the Accountant of Court to deliver up the bond of caution. The interlocutor sheet is transmitted to the Accountant (despite the *Practice Note* of May 14, 1970, which requires the process to be retransmitted). The Accountant delivers up the bond and the interlocutor sheet is returned to the process. The last interlocutor is usually extracted.

Petition for the appointment of a new curator bonis (the original curator having died) and for discharge of the deceased curator

This petition, as may be expected, combines features of the two previous curatory petitions. It is only necessary to indicate in outline the procedure, the details of which have been mentioned already.

When any petition is presented for a new appointment of a *curator bonis*, two new medical certificates are normally required to confirm the ward's incapacity, although occasionally in the past only one certificate or none has been sufficient. The procedure is not special until after there has been intimation and service. The first motion is, "On behalf of the petitioner to appoint —— to be *curator bonis* to ——, in terms of the prayer of the petition; and to remit to the Accountant of Court to report on the deceased *curator bonis's* intromissions with a view to his discharge (and for expenses)." The problem of expenses turns on the same point mentioned earlier (pp. 71 and 72). The process makes two visits to the Accountant. On the first occasion it is transmitted so that the new curator may find caution. It has to be retransmitted to the petition department so that a certified copy interlocutor of the new appointment can be prepared. After that, the process is taken back to the Accountant so that he may report on the deceased curator's intromissions. In the Accountant's report there will be a proposal that not only the deceased curator but also his representatives should be discharged. A motion is enrolled, "On behalf of the petitioner in respect of the report by the Accountant of Court number —— of process, for exoneration and discharge of the deceased *curator bonis* and his representatives in terms of the prayer of the petition." The appropriate interlocutor is passed.

Petition for recall of curatory and appointment of curator bonis (ward recovered)

This petition is usually presented by the ward. It is supported by two medical certificates which state that the ward is now capable of managing his affairs or giving instructions for their management. They should be in the same form as certificates of incapacity and they are repeated in the appendix to the petition. It is not insisted that the examinations should have taken place within 30 days prior to the presentation of the petition.

The petition with a certified copy is lodged in the original curatory process. As with other curatory petitions two copies are "boxed" and an order for intimation and service is granted without a motion being enrolled. Service will be on the *curator bonis*, relatives and the curator's cautioners. After an execution copy petition is lodged a motion is enrolled, "On behalf of the petitioner to recall the curatory and the appointment of —— as *curator bonis*, to remit to the Accountant of Court to report on the curator's intromissions with the estate with a view to his discharge (and to find the *curator bonis* entitled to his expenses out of the curatory estate)." The problem with expenses is mentioned earlier (pp. 71 and 72). An interlocutor is passed, the Accountant reports, and a motion is enrolled for discharge. The final interlocutor is often extracted.

Petition for recall of appointment of a curator bonis, for new appointment of a curator bonis and for discharge of the previous curator bonis

The procedure is similar to the other applications which involve both an appointment and a discharge. As with any petition for a new appointment, fresh medical certificates are usually needed to confirm the ward's incapacity. As the curator who no longer wishes to act is alive, his appointment must be recalled. After the execution copy petition is lodged a motion is enrolled, "On behalf of the petitioner to recall his appointment as *curator bonis*, to nominate and appoint —— to be *curator bonis* to —— in terms of the prayer of the petition, to remit to the Accountant of Court to report on the petitioner's intromissions with the estate with a view to his discharge (and for expenses)." The process makes two journeys to the Accountant. The first is when the new curator is finding caution. The process is returned to allow a certified copy of the appointment of the new curator to be prepared. The process goes back to the Accountant for a report on the discharge. The details of the stages can be found earlier in this chapter.

Petition for the appointment of a new curator bonis, the original curator bonis having been appointed in the sheriff court

The procedure has some marked differences from other curatory petitions. The petition starts with an order for intimation and service. The execution copy petition is lodged and a motion is enrolled, "On behalf of the petitioner to find that there is a contingency between this process and the process in the initial writ at the instance of —— for the appointment of a *curator bonis* to —— in the Sheriff Court of —— and to authorise the Sheriff Clerk of —— or his depute to transmit the Sheriff Court process to the Court of Session, 2 Parliament Square, Edinburgh." Once the sheriff court process has been remitted a motion is enrolled, "On behalf of the petitioner to conjoin this process and the Sheriff Court process *ob contingentiam,* for appointment of —— as *curator bonis* to ——; to remit to the Accountant of Court to report on the (deceased curator's or as the case may be) intromissions (and for expenses)." The necessary interlocutor is passed and the process is transmitted to the Accountant so that the new curator can find caution. The process is taken back to the petition department for the issue of a certified copy of the interlocutor which makes the new appointment and then retransmitted to the Accountant so that he can report on the request for a discharge. The Accountant reports and a motion is enrolled and granted to discharge the previous curator. Fuller details of the steps to be taken within this framework will be found earlier in this chapter where the general issues of appointment and discharge are considered.

Petition for appointment of a curator to a minor

There is considerable confusion about the circumstances in which it is competent to appoint a curator or *curator bonis* to a minor. The matter was examined by Sheriff N. M. L. Walker (*op. cit.*, pp. 15–20) and it is not appropriate in this short work to enter into an elaborate discussion of the authorities. The underlying law affects the procedure. A *curator bonis* supersedes a person in the management of his affairs and this appears an inappropriate step to take when the minor's only incapacity is his age. A curator to a minor has an established role. He consents to some of the acts of a minor and never acts in place of the minor. In this situation he is not a judicial factor, he need not find caution and he is not supervised by the Accountant of Court. The least controversial course is for the minor to present a petition under section 12 of the Administration of Justice (Scotland) Act 1933. This is a simple petition which is intimated and served and a motion is enrolled to grant the prayer of the petition. There is no award of expenses unless a party opposes the petition. Jurisdiction will be governed by section 16 of the Family Law Act 1986 when the Act is in force.

CHAPTER 10

FOREIGN JUDGMENTS

Introduction

A foreign judgment may be enforced in Scotland by following various statutory procedures. The basis of these procedures is the registration of the foreign decree in the books of a Scottish court followed by enforcement as if it were a Scottish decree. The problem of which decrees may be enforced is very complex and cannot be dealt with here. The reader is referred to two works by Professor A. E. Anton, namely, *Private International Law* (1967), Chap. 26 and *Civil Jurisdiction in Scotland* (1984) and to a useful article by Professor R. Black, "Enforcement of Scottish Decrees Outside Scotland and of Non-Scottish Decrees Within Scotland" (1987) 32 J.L.S. 10.

The court in which a judgment is to be enforced will have exclusive jurisdiction to hear the application. There is specific statutory provision to this effect in the Civil Jurisdiction and Judgments Act 1982, Sched 1, art. 16; Sched, 4, section 5; and Sched, 8, para. 4 (1) (*d*).

Common law

The common law procedure to enforce a foreign decree is to seek a decree conform. This is a procedure by way of summons. The case proceeds like an ordinary action for payment, but founded on the foreign decree. This procedure cannot be used to enforce some United Kingdom judgments because of section 18 (8) of the Civil Jurisdiction and Judgments Act 1982 nor can it be used to enforce a decree to which the Foreign Judgments (Reciprocal Enforcement) Act 1933 applies (s. 6, 1933 Act). If a decree conform is sought when the Administration of Justice Act 1920 applies, there may be a penalty because expenses might not be obtained (s. 9 (5), 1920 Act). A judgment obtained in another Contracting State (see p. 14) and falling within the scope of the 1968 Convention, should be enforced only under the Convention (*i.e.* under the Civil Jurisdiction and Judgments Act 1982). See *De Wolf* v. *Cox* (42/76) [1976] E.C.R. 1759 and Anton, *Civil Jurisdiction*, para. 8.10.

Statutory procedures

The nationality of the court which granted the judgment affects the procedure which is used. A judgment for a money debt which has been awarded by a superior court of certain of Her Majesty's Dominions may be enforced under the Administration of Justice Act 1920. If the money judgment is from another foreign country it may be possible to enforce it under the Foreign Judgments (Reciprocal Enforcement) Act 1933. If the judgment is of a court of the United Kingdom or of another EEC country and is a judgment in a civil and commercial matter it is probable that the Civil Jurisdiction and Judgments Act 1982 applies. For the sake of completeness it should be added that maintenance judgments are in a special position and can be enforced in the sheriff court (see the Maintenance Orders Act 1950 and the Maintenance Orders (Reciprocal Enforcement) Act 1972 which are not affected by the U.K. scheme in the 1982 Act as a result of sections 18 (5) and (7) of the 1982 Act; but the 1982 Act may be used as an alternative for an EEC maintenance order, see Anton, *Civil Jurisdiction,* paras. 8.53–8.55). The international aspects of child abduction are considered in Chapter 5.

A list of the countries to which the 1920 and 1933 Acts apply will be found in the article by Professor Black cited earlier. The application of the 1933 Act to Dominions was considered in *Jamieson* v. *Northern Electricity Supply Corporation (Private) Ltd.,* 1970 S.L.T. 113.

The rules of court which apply to applications to the Court of Session are sufficiently detailed for repetition of all their terms to be otiose. In general the provisions for registration of foreign judgments seek to have a simple system which, in the first instance, does not require service on the debtor, but which allows the debtor to intervene and argue that the court should not give recognition to the judgment. The ultimate aim of the applicant is registration of the judgment in the Books of Council and Session and its enforcement by diligence.

Administration of Justice Act 1920

Procedure is by petition to the Outer House under rule 248. The petition is accompanied by the judgment or a certified copy and an affidavit. There is no order at this stage for intimation and service. An interlocutor authorises the Keeper of the Registers of Scotland to register the judgment upon production of a certified copy of the interlocutor. The interlocutor specifies a date before which the debtor can challenge the registration. The date would normally relate to the period of time which would be the *induciae* for service in the country concerned. Intimation is made to the debtor and an execution of intimation lodged in process. Extract of the registered judgment is superseded until a certificate is granted by the Deputy Principal Clerk that no application has been made to have the registration set aside or that any such application has been refused.

The Act also applies to the enforcement of a Court of Session judgment in the Dominions, Rule 248 (*h*) has a simple procedure by petition for obtaining a certified copy of a Court of Session judgment for enforcement abroad.

Foreign Judgments (Reciprocal Enforcement) Act 1933

Procedure is by petition to the Outer House under rule 249. Procedure is similar to a petition under the 1920 Act except that there are elaborate provisions on the content of the affidavit and the form of the notice of intimation to be given to the debtor.

The certificate obtained to enforce a Court of Session judgment under the Act is more elaborate than under the 1920 Act.

Civil Jurisdiction and Judgments Act 1982

The 1982 Act, which came into force on January 1, 1987, repealed the Judgments Extension Act 1868 which was the Act commonly used to enforce the judgments of superior courts in England and Northern Ireland. The 1982 Act repealed also the Inferior Courts Judgments Extension Act 1882 with the result that enforcement is channelled to the superior courts of the United Kingdom with the exception of maintenance orders.

The 1982 Act applies to a judgment of a court or tribunal of a Contracting State (see Art. 25 of the 1986 Convention in Sched. 1 to the 1982 Act). The judgment must be in a civil or commercial matter which is not excluded by Article 1. The details of the application of the Act will be found in Professor Anton's book on *Civil Jurisdiction*. The procedure for enforcement of a judgment is set out in rules 249D to 249R (added by Act of Sederunt (Rules of Court Amendment No. 9) (Jurisdiction and Enforcement) 1986; S.I. 1986 No. 1941).

The enforcement under section 4 of a judgment of a court or tribunal of a Contracting State is regulated by rules 249E to 249M. (These rules are annotated in the Supplement (1987) to Anton, *Civil Jurisdiction.*) The procedure is by application on Form 53 to the petition department with a process (the rules do not specifically require a process but some of the rules are difficult to operate without one. See, for example, rules 249E (3) (*a*) and 249L). The procedure differs notably from that under the 1920 and 1933 Acts in the following respects:

(a) The application is on a prescribed form (Form 53);

(b) The application may be signed by the applicant (rule 249E (1) (*b*) (i);

(c) Any hearing required under rule 249F shall be in chambers;

(d) The court, in addition to granting warrant to register the judgment, grants decree in terms of the judgment and, where necessary, grants decree in accordance with Scots law (rule 249G (1)). This is necessary because the reciprocal arrangements apply to non-money judgements;

(e) The applicant may apply for authority to do diligence or take protective measures before the time for appeal has expired (rule 249G (3);

(f) The decree can be registered immediately and extract can be obtained any time after registration.

The enforcement of a money judgment of another United Kingdom court or tribunal under section 18 of the Act involves the production to the Keeper of the Registers of a certificate issued in England or Northern Ireland under Schedule 6 (rule 249P (2)). In normal circumstances the court is not involved, although there can be a petition to sist proceedings or reduce a registration. There is a six-month time limit for registration of the certificate but more than one certificate can be obtained (Sched. 6, para. 4 (2)).

The enforcement of a non-money judgment of another United Kingdom court or tribunal uses Form 58 and this is dealt with by a judge (see rule 249Q (4) to (8); on the reasons for the different treatment of non-money orders see Anton, *op. cit.*, para. 9.38).

The rules contain provisions relating to the enforcement elsewhere of a Court of Session decree or a writ registered in the Books of Council and Session (rules 249N to Q).

Insolvency Act 1986

Section 18 (3) (*c*) of the Civil Jurisdiction and Judgments Act 1982 makes it clear that the provisions on enforcement of United Kingdom judgments in other parts of the United Kingdom do not apply to proceedings relating to bankruptcy or winding up. A similar exclusion applies to the Convention (Art. 1; but see the limited scope given to this by Anton, *op. cit.*, para. 3.20). Under section 426 of the Insolvency Act 1986 an order made by a court in any part of the United Kingdom in relation to insolvency matters shall be enforced in any other part of the United Kingdom as if it were an order of a court in that part of the United Kingdom subject to certain exceptions (s. 426 (2)).

Child abduction and child custody

The statutory provisions which deal with enforcement and recognition of orders made by courts outside Scotland are mentioned in Chapter 5.

European Community judgments

A Community judgment may be registered in a register kept by the Deputy Principal Clerk of Session. The application for registration is made by petition to the Outer House and the procedure is regulated by rules 296F to 296K. "Community judgment" is rather narrowly defined in rule 296F.

CHAPTER 11

FORFEITURE ACT

Introduction

As a general rule a person cannot benefit from his own crime with the result that a person cannot, at common law, succeed to the estate of someone whom he has killed (*Smith, Petr.*, 1979 S.L.T.(Sh.Ct.) 35; *Burns* v. *Secretary of State for Social Services*, 1985 S.L.T. 351). This rule applies to death caused by murder and (except, perhaps, in very exceptional cases) to death caused by culpable homicide. It may be doubted whether the rule applies when the "crime" is a statutory crime of the nature of careless driving or a breach of health and safety legislation. In these cases there is an absence of an intention to be violent.

There is a statutory provision in the Parricide Act 1594 which disinherits anyone who is convicted of killing a parent or grandparent. Relief from the common law rule which prevents inheritance (but not from the Parricide Act?) can be obtained under the Forfeiture Act 1982. Section 2 of the Forfeiture Act provides that the court may modify the forfeiture rule in a case of unlawful killing, whether or not there is a conviction. "Unlawful killing" is not defined but the Act extends to those who are art and part in the killing (s. 1 (2)). The Act does not apply in the case of a person convicted of murder (s. 5).

The procedure under the 1982 Act is by petition to the Outer House, although where testamentary provisions required to be considered it might be necessary to have a declarator (*Paterson, Petr.*, 1986 S.L.T. 121). Proceedings must be brought within three months from the date of a conviction, if any (s. 2 (3); *Re Royse (dec'd)* [1985] Ch. 22). The court has a wide discretion in modifying the effect of the forfeiture rule (*Re K (dec'd)* [1986] Ch. 180).

Jurisdiction

The jurisdiction rules in the Civil Jurisdiction and Judgments Act 1982 apply in only a modified way to matters relating to succession. The 1968 Convention does not apply to wills and succession (Sched. 1, art. 1). This excludes similar proceedings from the inter-United Kingdom in Schedule 4 (s. 16 (1) (*a*)). But it appears that the Scottish rules of jurisdiction in Schedule 8 apply to proceedings relating to succession, other than Commissary proceedings (Sched. 9, para. 7).

Procedure

The procedure narrated is based on *Cross, Petr.*, 1987 S.L.T. 384. In that case it was decided by Lord Cowie that a complete exemption from the forfeiture rule was not competent.

1. A petition is lodged with a copy for the Advocates' Library, a process and an inventory of productions and productions. The productions might include an extract of a conviction for culpable homicide and a valuation of property. Service is sought on those who are interested in the estate and on the Lord Advocate. The prayer of the petition seeks an order which modifies the forfeiture rule by allowing the petitioner to acquire such interest in the estate of the deceased as to the court appears proper. Without a motion being enrolled there will be an interlocutor for intimation and service.

2. An execution copy petition is lodged. Assuming that answers have not been lodged a motion is enrolled, "On behalf of the petitioner for an order for a hearing." The interlocutor appoints the cause to a hearing and a date is fixed by the petitioner's solicitor with the Keeper of the Rolls. The Crown may wish to be informed of the date of the hearing by the petition department.

3. At the hearing counsel argue for a modification of the forfeiture rule. The interlocutor may exclude certain property from the operation of the rule.

CHAPTER 12

INHIBITION

Introduction

An application for letters of inhibition used to commence in the petition department. The procedure and the nature of inhibition is explained in the first edition of this book (pp. 45–48). But as from March 1, 1986 all applications for fiats must be lodged in the signeting office of the general department (*Practice Note* of February 21, 1986). The result is that the petition department are no longer involved in the grant of letters of inhibition. A *caveat* against an inhibition (see p. 6) should be lodged with the petition department. The main concern of the petition department with inhibitions arises with petitions for recall.

An inhibition prescribes in five years unless renewed (Conveyancing (Scotland) Act 1924, s. 44 (3) (*a*)). The inhibition may be discharged following an express discharge by the creditor (*Encyclopaedia of Scottish Legal Styles*, Vol. 5, p. 373; G. L. Gretton, *The Law of Inhibition and Adjudication* (1987) pp. 31 and 174). There was doubt about the period of prescription of an inhibition of a wife's *praepositura* (E. M. Clive, *The Law of Husband and Wife in Scotland* (2nd ed., 1982), pp. 272, 273) but this is of little practical importance following on the abolition of this form of inhibition by the Law Reform (Husband and Wife) (Scotland) Act 1984, s. 7 (2).

Section 27 (1) (*b*) of the Civil Jurisdiction and Judgments Act 1982 allows the court to grant warrant of inhibition in any case in which proceedings have commenced in another Contracting State or in England, Wales or Northern Ireland. Until now these applications have been presented as petitions in the Outer House. It does not appear normal to proceed to apply for letters of inhibition, presumably because of doubt as to whether a foreign writ is a competent ground for the issue of letters.

Recall and restriction

An application for recall of an inhibition may be sought:

(a) By motion in an existing process (rule 74 (*h*). This is the appropriate procedure, except in exceptional cases, in respect of an inhibition granted in an action before the court (*Stuart* v. *Stuart*, 1926 S.L.T. 31; *Beton* v. *Beton*, 1961 S.L.T. (Notes) 19). If the application is made before the case has called a letter is addressed to the Deputy Principal Clerk and the procedure in rule 74 (*g*) is followed. The court may also recall an inhibition when disposing of a case in which a joint minute has been lodged (*Barbour's Tr.* v. *Davidsons* (1878) 15 S.L.R. 438 and *Encyclopaedia of Scottish Legal Styles*, Vol. 5, p. 371)).

(b) By petition under the *nobile officium* to the Inner House. This may be appropriate, for example, if the inhibition was granted on a summons and the process has been finally extracted.

(c) By petition to the Outer House under rule 189 (*a*) (xv). This applies to an inhibition which was granted on a bill or a bill for letters. It will therefore apply to inhibitions which were granted on bills which proceeded on a sheriff court writ. This type of petition has become relatively common and the procedure is explained below.

An inhibition may be partially recalled so that it remains over some, but not all, the heritage (*McInally* v. *Kildonan Homes Ltd.*, 1979 S.L.T. (Notes) 89). Inhibition also can be granted with a restriction on the heritage to which it applies (*Pow* v. *Pow*, 1987 S.L.T. 127). A substantial percentage of the petitions for recall are presented to obtain restriction of the inhibition. The procedure in the Outer House petition is as follows:

1. A petition is lodged with a process and a copy of the petition for the Advocates' Library. There will be an inventory of productions with productions which are the deeds founded on in the petition (rule 194). The productions may include a certified copy initial writ, letters of inhibition, a search in the register of inhibitions and adjudications, and a certified copy of any relevant interlocutor. If partial recall or restriction is sought there may be a surveyor's report on the value of property.

2. A practice has arisen recently, in a small number of cases, in which a motion for interim recall of an inhibition has been enrolled and granted, in one instance before intimation and service of the petition. There must be serious doubts about the competence of this procedure. There must either be a recall or not and once a recall is granted property may be sold. It is thought that the Register of Inhibitions and Adjudications cannot show some form of temporary lifting of the inhibition. In any event it is a very drastic measure to recall an inhibition on an *ex parte* statement made without any opportunity being given to the inhibiter to oppose the motion.

3. Without enrolling a motion an interlocutor is granted which allows intimation and service. In a number of cases the court has

granted a motion to reduce the *induciae* where missives were about to be completed in relation to the property. Service will be on the creditor. If answers are lodged the petition will proceed as an opposed petition (see p. 12). Consignation (see p. 16) or caution may be made a condition for recall (*cf. David McAlpine Properties Ltd.* v. *Jack Jarvis (Kirkcaldy) Ltd.*, 1987 G.W.D. 16–620). In the absence of answers an execution copy petition is lodged and a motion enrolled to grant the prayer of the petition. If the inhibition is to be recalled completely the interlocutor is in this form:

> "The Lord Ordinary, having resumed consideration of the Petition, no answers having been lodged, recalls the inhibition used at the instance of the respondents against the petitioner and recorded in the Register of Inhibitions and Adjudications on [date] and grants authority for a certified copy of this interlocutor to be recorded in said Register."

If the inhibition is to be restricted the interlocutor is in this form:

> "The Lord Ordinary, having resumed consideration of the Petition, no answers having been lodged, restricts the inhibition used at the instance of the respondents against the petitioner which was registered in the Register of Inhibitions and Adjudications on [date] to the dwelling-house at ——— belonging to the petitioner and grants authority for a certified copy of this interlocutor to be recorded in said register."

3. The petitioner's solicitor obtains a certified copy of the interlocutor for recording and he or she may also borrow the productions.

CHAPTER 13

JUDICIAL FACTOR

Introduction

The grounds on which a judicial factor may be appointed are varied, which makes it difficult to generalise on the petition procedure. As a general rule it can be assumed that the procedures which apply to a petition for a *curator bonis* apply to a judicial factor (see Chapter 9). The appointment of a judicial factor may be inappropriate if there are disputed and difficult questions which should be decided by another procedure such as declarator (*Heggie* v. *Davidson*, 1973 S.L.T. (Notes) 47).

Rule 189 (*a*) (i) provides that petitions "for the appointment of judicial factors, factors *loco tutoris*, or *loco absentis*, factors pending litigation, or *curator bonis* to a minor or *incapax*" are Outer House petitions. Similarly treated are factors on the estates of partnerships or joint ventures (rule 189 (*a*) (ii)). There is an exception in the case of a judicial factor on the estate of a solicitor under the Solicitors (Scotland) Act 1980. This, being a petition under the Acts relating to solicitors, is an Inner House petition (rule 190 (iv); and see p. 136).

Jurisdiction

Questions of jurisdiction can be very complicated and much depends on the type of judicial factor involved. The result may reflect the uncertainties which apply to curatory petitions (p. 61) or the rules which apply in company petitions (p. 52) or sequestrations (p. 123) or trusts (p. 148). Problems which concern the dissolution of a company or a partnership may be subject to the exclusive jurisdiction of the Scottish courts when the body concerned has its seat in Scotland. This is the effect of the Civil Jurisdiction and Judgments Act 1982, Sched. 1, art. 16; Sched. 4, s. 5; Sched. 8, para. 4 (1) (*b*). On the meaning of "seat" see A. E. Anton, *Civil Jurisdiction in Scotland* (1984), paras. 4.22–4.34.

Sequestration

The appointment of a judicial factor usually involves also the sequestration of estates. Because "sequestration" is in common use in the context of bankruptcy it is sometimes, wrongly, assumed that sequestration implies insolvency. Sequestration is a judicial order which removes property from the control of its possessor. The property is then administered by a factor who is appointed by the court. If the court merely appointed a factor it would not remove the power of those already in charge of the property. Sequestration is necessary to remove the estate from the control of its possessor. So a petition will usually seek sequestration followed by the appointment of a judicial factor (*Booth* v. *Mackinnon* (1908) 15 S.L.T. 848; N. M. L. Walker, *Judicial Factors*, p. 4).

Statutory and other rules

Various statutes apply to judicial factors. The most important for present purposes are the Judicial Factors Act 1849 and the Judicial Factors (Scotland) Act 1889. A judicial factor is a trustee in terms of the Trusts (Scotland) Acts 1921 and 1961. *Notes for the Guidance of Judicial Factors* are issued by the Accountant of Court. Rules of Court 199 to 201 apply to factors.

Procedure

Most of the procedure applicable to a *curator bonis* applies to other factors (see Chapter 9). This is particularly true of the appointment of a factor *loco tutoris* who automatically becomes a *curator bonis* to a minor (1889 Act, s. 11) until the minor reaches the age of 18 (*McIntosh* v. *Wood*, 1970 S.C. 179). A factor on a trust estate appears to be relatively uncommon probably because in most cases it will be better to appoint new trustees (for which see p. 149). This chapter mentions some of the specialities which apply on the appointment of a factor to a partnership or company estate and on the estate of a deceased person. On removal of a factor see *Dunlop, Petr.*, 1987 G.W.D. 12–424.

Caution

It is still necessary for a judicial factor to find caution. There is a time limit for finding caution (rule 200 (*c*)). The procedure for finding caution is set out in rule 200. In a sequestration on bankruptcy under the Bankruptcy (Scotland) Act 1985 and in insolvency proceedings under the Insolvency Act 1986 it is no longer necessary to lodge a bond of caution in process, but these procedures do not apply to a judicial factory.

Factor on partnership estate

Two slightly different situations arise in practice. The court may be asked to dissolve the partnership under section 35 of the Partnership Act 1890 and then appoint a factor. Alternatively the partnership may be dissolved already and a factor is needed to wind up the firm under section 39 of the 1890 Act (*e.g. Carabine* v. *Carabine*, 1949 S.C. 521). A factor may be appointed on an interim basis as was decided in *McCulloch* v. *McCulloch*, 1953 S.C. 189 and interim appointments are not as rare as that case might suggest. On the contrary, there is now nothing unusual in an interim appointment. The procedure for an interim appointment follows that in a curatory petition (p. 64) although the interlocutor sequestrates the estate before appointing the factor *ad interim*.

The interlocutor which makes a permanent appointment of a factor varies according to whether or not the partnership has been dissolved. If it has not been dissolved the interlocutor states:

> "The Lord Ordinary, having heard counsel, dissolves the partnership and for that purpose sequestrates the estates of the firm known as —— ; Nominates and Appoints X (design) to be judicial factor with the usual powers on the estates of the said firm; authorises the said X after finding caution to enter upon the duties of his office upon a certified copy of this interlocutor; appoints intimation of the dissolution of the partnership to be made in the *Edinburgh Gazette* and —— newspapers; finds the petitioner entitled to all of his expenses out of the partnership estate and remits the accounts thereof when lodged to the Auditor of Court to tax and report."

If the partnership has been dissolved already the reference to dissolution is omitted and there need be no advertisement of the order. Otherwise the procedure is similar to the appointment of a *curator bonis*. On the meaning of "usual powers" see *Carmichael's J. F.* v. *Accountant of Court*, 1971 S.C. 295 and N. M. L. Walker, *Judicial Factors*, p. 39.

Factor on company estate

It was established in *Fraser, Petr.*, 1971 S.L.T. 146 that it was competent to appoint a judicial factor *ad interim* on the estate of a company incorporated under the Companies Acts and that this was an Outer House petition. The procedure is very similar to a petition for a factor on a partnership estate. The two differences are that the appointment of a factor has to be intimated to the Registrar of Companies and advertised in the *Edinburgh Gazette*.

Factor on a deceased person's estate

An appointment of a factor on a deceased person's estate may be made under section 11A of the Judicial Factors (Scotland) Act

1889, which was added by Schedule 7 to the Bankruptcy (Scotland) Act 1985. The procedure is regulated in some detail by rule 201. The assumption is that the estate is, or may be, insolvent. This is the reason that the procedure differs from the appointment of other judicial factors. There is a need to protect the interests of creditors. An alternative to the appointment of a judicial factor is sequestration of the estate under section 5 (3) of the Bankruptcy (Scotland) Act 1985. But the category of person who may petition under section 5 (3) is slightly narrower than those who may petition under section 11A of the Judicial Factors (Scotland) Act 1889. The procedure under the Judicial Factors Act is most useful when there is doubt about whether the estate is insolvent. If it turns out that the estate is solvent, the factor can distribute it to those who are entitled to it (rule 201 (*o*)). It is not so clear that a permanent trustee could do this.

An executor who knows or who ought to have known that the estate was absolutely insolvent should petition for sequestration or the appointment of a judicial factor within a reasonable time. If he does not do so he is a vitious intromitter and may be liable for some or all of the debts of the deceased (Bankruptcy (Scotland) Act 1985, s. 8 (4)).

If an estate is both sequestrated under the Bankruptcy (Scotland) Act and a judicial factor is appointed, section 10 of the 1985 Act provides a mechanism to regulate the conflict.

The procedure for appointment of a factor is as follows:

1. A petition is presented with a copy for the Advocates' Library and a copy for the Accountant of Court (rule 200 (*a*)). The rules provide a form of petition (Form 29). The productions will be an extract decree or other voucher which establishes the debt or other evidence of interest in the estate.

2. There will be a first order for intimation advertisement and service. The form of the advertisement in the *Edinburgh Gazette* is Form 31.

3. An execution copy petition is lodged with an inventory of productions and a copy of the *Gazette* which contains the advertisement. Unless an interim appointment is to be made the appointment of the judicial factor cannot take place until the lapse of 14 days, or such other time as the court may fix, after the appearance of the advertisement and after the date of service on the representatives of the deceased (rule 201 (*c*)). As the *induciae* which governs petitions is now 21 days (rule 192), the *induciae* following advertisement will probably be 21 days. A motion is enrolled to grant the prayer of the petition with expenses. An interlocutor will be signed which appoints the judicial factor and

allows him, after finding caution, to enter on his duties upon a certified copy of the interlocutor.

4. The process is transmitted to the Accountant of Court so that caution may be found (see p. 66). When caution is found and the process is returned to the petition department a certified copy of the interlocutor is made up for the solicitor and issued to him.

5. Within 14 days of the issue of the certified copy interlocutor the factor must insert in the *Edinburgh Gazette* and other appropriate newspapers, a notice in the prescribed form which calls for claims (rule 201 (*d*)). The notice calls for claims to be lodged within four months.

6. Within six months of the issue of the certified copy interlocutor the factor must lodge with the Accountant of Court an inventory of the estate and a report on the debts (rule 201 (*f*); the period is six months from the date the Accountant receives the bond of caution under section 3 of the Judicial Factors Act 1849).

7. The factor proceeds to realise the estate. He must reserve out of the first funds realised sufficient to defray the cost of administration. He may pay certain privileged debts, but not others, without first lodging a scheme of division with the Accountant (rule 201 (*n*)).

8. A procedure is provided for making a partial payment to creditors (rule 201 (*m*)). In an insolvent estate the valuation of creditors' claims and the distribution of the estate follow the rules in the Bankruptcy (Scotland) Act 1985 (1889 Act, s. 11A (2)). The factor adjudicates on claims and lodges annual accounts with the Accountant until he is in a position to lodge with the Accountant a State of Funds and Scheme of Division. If, however, there are no creditors the factor prepares a surplus report (rules 201 (*g*) and 201 (*o*)). If there are no funds available after payment of debts, a State of Funds only is prepared (rule 201 (*g*)). In practice if the factor is to pay a dividend to creditors he will be asked to lodge an interim account so that this may be audited and the amount of his commission fixed. If it is anticipated that there may be a surplus it is not so necessary to estimate the sum due for closing expenses.

9. A State of Funds and Scheme of Division is lodged with the Accountant. This is reported on by the Accountant and lodged in process with the Accountant's report, the factor's inventory and accounts and the Accountant's audit reports to date. The solicitor for the factor should advise the factor to make the intimations to creditors and to insert the *Gazette* notice as provided in rule 201 (*h*). There is a three-week period for objections to be lodged (rule 201 (*j*)). A certificate is signed by the factor which confirms

that notices have been sent. A style for this certificate is in Chapter 26. The certificate is lodged in process with copies of the notices and a copy of the *Gazette* which contained the advertisement.

10. On the expiry of the three-week period a motion may be enrolled for approval of the scheme and after approval the solicitor for the factor should inform the factor that he may distribute the sums allocated in the scheme of division (rule 201 (*l*)). If there is a surplus after paying creditors the court, instead of authorising the factor to pay the surplus, may direct the factor to continue to administer the surplus. This normally happens when the beneficiary is under-age and, as appears from the Accountant's report, it is advisable that supervision over the fund should continue or, it may be, that a multiplepoinding is needed to decide who owns the estate (rule 201 (*o*)).

11. The factor lodges a consignation receipt for unclaimed dividends with the Accountant (see p. 16). The factor needs to obtain from the Inland Revenue a certificate that all taxes have been paid (rule 36). For each payment to a creditor he must be able to produce a receipt from the creditor. If the receipt is signed by the creditor's solicitor or other agent, the Accountant will require to see the agent's mandate. When the factor has prepared a draft of his final account he is in a position to seek his discharge.

12. The discharge proceeds on a petition in terms of rule 201 (*p*). This provides for service on the representatives of the deceased and on the factor's cautioner. There must be advertisement in the *Edinburgh Gazette* in terms of Form 34. A period of 14 days must lapse from service and notice before the petition is disposed of. (In practice the normal 21-day *induciae* may be required.) An execution copy petition is lodged in process and a copy of the relevant *Gazette* and an inventory of productions. The petition department clerk will check, in particular, that the advertisement followed Form 34.

13. There is a remit to the Accountant to report and it follows the same course as the discharge of a *curator bonis* (see Chapter 9) except that the Accountant will require the taxed and receipted account of the expenses of the discharge to be exhibited to him prior to the completion of his discharge report. This is so that the Accountant may ensure that funds retained by the factor to meet closing expenses have been fully expended.

14. As in the case of a curatory, the judicial factory may be written off if the factor is willing to dispense with judicial discharge or if the factor makes no application for a discharge. In those cases, however, delivery of the bond of caution is not made.

Chapter 14

JUDICIAL REVIEW

Introduction

The procedure for judicial review was introduced with effect from April 30, 1985 by Act of Sederunt (Rules of Court Amendment No. 2) (Judicial Review) 1985 (S.I. 1985 No. 500). The procedure is governed by rule 260B. What follows is a description of the practice of the court. There are many other issues which might be raised by judicial review. Some of these are discussed in J. St. Clair and N. F. Davidson, *Judicial Review in Scotland* (1986) and in "Administrative Law," in the *Stair Memorial Encyclopaedia*, Vol. 1, paras. 348–400.

Problems of title and interest to sue have arisen (see, for example, *Scottish Old People's Welfare Council, Petrs.*, 1987 S.L.T. 179; *Lothian Building Preservation Trust* v. *Midlothian D.C.*, March 26, 1987, P27/12/87; and *Patmor Ltd.* v. *City of Edinburgh Licensing Board*, 1987 S.L.T. 492). Most of the respondents have been local authorities, the Secretary of State or licensing boards. Many issues remain unsettled about which bodies are subject to judicial review and in what circumstances (see St. Clair and Davidson, *op. cit.*, para. 3.16 *et seq.*; P. Robson, "Judicial Review and Homelessness," 1985 S.L.T. (News) 305).

Some cases are decided with little reference to case authority. Reported cases which are often referred to are *Associated Provincial Picture Houses Ltd.* v. *Wednesbury Corp.* [1948] 1 K.B. 223; *Brown* v. *Hamilton D.C.*, 1983 S.L.T. 397; *Wordie Property Co. Ltd.* v. *Secretary of State for Scotland*, 1984 S.L.T. 345; *Council of Civil Service Unions* v. *Minister for the Civil Service* [1985] A.C. 374, esp. *per* Lord Diplock at p. 408; and *Puhlhofer* v. *Hillingdon London B.C.* [1986] A.C. 484.

An issue which is arising, and has yet to be settled, is the competence of an application for judicial review when there is another remedy. Lord Jauncey has observed:

"I must deal with a point of competency argued with some force by the respondents.

It is perhaps sometimes forgotten by litigants that the Rule of Court 260B, which instituted the expedited procedure for judicial review, provides no remedy or relief which did not already exist. The supervisory jurisdiction of the Court of Session will continue to be exercised only in those cases in which it could have been exercised before the rule was introduced. That jurisdiction is not available as a general mode of appeal against decisions of tribunals or other bodies but is rather available in limited circumstances where no other means of review exist (*Brown* v. *Hamilton D.C.*, 1983 S.L.T. 397 per Lord Fraser of Tullybelton at p. 414). It is certainly not available where other means of review are provided and those means have either not been made use of or have been used without success (*Adair* v. *Colville & Sons*, 1926 S.C.(H.L.) 51 per Viscount Dunedin at p. 56)."

(*O'Neill* v. *Scottish Joint Negotiating Committee for Teaching Staff in School Education*, 1987 S.C.L.R. 275 at p. 277; *cf. Nahar* v. *Strathclyde R.C.*, 1986 S.L.T. 570; *Sleigh* v. *Edinburgh D.C.*, 1987 G.W.D. 13–465.)

The extent to which there may be qualifications to the view expressed by Lord Jauncey remains to be explored in future cases. *British Railways Board* v. *Glasgow Corporation*, 1976 S.C. 224 suggests that some qualifications may exist (see also C. M. G. Himsworth, "Defining the Boundaries of Judicial Review," 1985 S.L.T. (News) 369; S. L. Stuart, "Judicial Review and Alternative Remedies," 1986 S.L.T. (News) 309).

The position is thought to be different where the petition seeks an order for restoration of property or specific performance under section 91 of the Court of Session Act 1868. The existence of an alternative remedy is not a bar to a remedy under section 91 (*T. Docherty Ltd.* v. *Burgh of Monifieth*, 1970 S.C. 200; *Walker* v. *Strathclyde R.C. (No. 1)*, 1986 S.L.T. 523). A petition under section 91 now follows judicial review procedure (rule 260B (2)).

Procedure

In a simple case the procedure followed is:

1. A petition is lodged with a copy for the Advocates' Library, a process, an inventory of productions and productions. The petition is in form 39A. The form of petition is unusual because there are pleas-in-law and the petition may incorporate legal argument and have a schedule of documents. Documents should either be lodged with the petition or a schedule to the petition may disclose who holds the documents (rules 260B (8) and (9)). Affidavits may be lodged. It has been observed: "The use of affidavits as a substitute for oral evidence is recognised by the act of sederunt dealing with judicial review but it may not be appropriate to deal with contentious issues of fact or opinion even although the affidavits may be amplified, as occurred in the

present case, by ex parte statements relative to matters raised at the hearing by parties or by the court." (*Walker* v. *Strathclyde R.C. (No. 2)*, 1987 S.L.T. 81 at pp. 81 and 82 *per* Lord Morison.)

2. The petition department clerk checks whether or not a *caveat* has been lodged. On the competence of a *caveat* see *Kelly* v. *Monklands D.C.*, 1986 S.L.T. 165.

3. In the absence of a *caveat* a motion is enrolled, "On behalf of the petitioner for an order for intimation and service and an order for a hearing." Counsel must be instructed. An interim order and other orders may be made at this stage (rule 260B (11)). The motion need not appear in the motion roll.

4. If the motion is granted there will be the first interlocutor. The terms of this interlocutor have varied in practice. According to one view (expressed by Lord Ross in *Kelly* v. *Monklands D.C.*, *sup. cit.*) the interlocutor should include an order for answers. The other view, and the one at present followed, is that the interlocutor need not require answers. Any person who intends to appear at the first hearing intimates that intention to the Keeper of the Rolls and the petitioner's solicitor 48 hours before the diet. Answers *may* be lodged (rule 260B (13)). Usually answers are lodged and it has been known for answers to be lodged at the bar at the first hearing. At that hearing there may be an order for answers (rule 260B (16) (*b*) (i)). The terms of the first interlocutor usually are:

> "The Lord Ordinary, having heard counsel, there being no *caveat*, Appoints the Petition to be intimated on the walls and in the minute book in common form and to be served as craved together with a copy of this interlocutor upon the persons named and designed in the schedule for service annexed to the Petition; Assigns [date] as the date for the First Hearing in the cause, said Hearing to take place within the Court of Session, 2 Parliament Square, Edinburgh, at ten o'clock forenoon; Appoints any party intending to appear at said Hearing to intimate such intention to the solicitors for the petitioner and the Keeper of the Rolls, 2 Parliament Square, Edinburgh, not later than 48 hours before the date of said hearing."

Intimation and service of this order should be carried out "immediately" (rule 260B (12)). The clerk of court will consult with the Keeper of the Rolls about the date for the first hearing. If there are difficulties in an estimation of the duration of the hearing (and there usually are) or a full debate is anticipated, the petitioner's solicitor may fix the time with the Keeper.

5. An execution copy petition is lodged. The judge at the first hearing has to satisfy himself that the terms of the first interlocutor have been complied with (rule 260B (15)). The parties are heard at the first hearing. In many cases the application is decided at, or shortly after, the first hearing. The Lord Ordinary can take the case to avizandum or, in a matter of urgency, give his decision and later issue his opinion. But it is possible for many other courses to be taken. There may be an order for answers at this time. There may be an order for documents or affidavits. A petition has been continued so that the petitioner could specify in the petition the legal authorities which were being relied upon. There may be an interim order or an order for further procedure. A list of the possible orders is in rule 260B (16).

6. One result of the first hearing can be an order for a second hearing. But this is not a common result. If more detail is wished the first hearing can be continued. If there is to be a second hearing the procedure in rules 260B (17) to (20) is followed. There can be a proof leading to an award of damages (*Kelly* v. *Monklands D.C.*, 1986 S.L.T. 169; *Mallon* v. *Monklands D.C.*, 1986 S.L.T. 347).

7. An order which determines the application may be reclaimed without leave. Any other order needs leave which must be applied for within seven days (rule 260B (21) and (22); *Kelly* v. *Monklands D.C.*, 1986 S.L.T. 165 at pp. 167 and 168, *per* Lord Ross). The procedure for reclaiming is explained at p. 19.

CHAPTER 15

LETTER OF REQUEST

Introduction

A civil court or tribunal outside Scotland can request that the Court of Session makes an order for evidence to be obtained in Scotland (Evidence (Proceedings in Other Jurisdictions) Act 1975). The application is a petition which is usually presented by the Lord Advocate. Some petitions have been presented by Edinburgh solicitors on behalf of a foreign court (*e.g. Knox, Petr.*, P7/13/87). Under previous legislation an application by an individual was allowed (*Stemrich, Petr.* (1886) 13 R. 1156; *McCorquodale*, 1923 S.C. 792). It was suggested at one time that when the Lord Advocate presented the petition the court would remit to a sheriff to take the evidence. But when an individual applied the court should appoint a member of the Bar to be the commissioner because the court had no right to add to the duties of a sheriff unless the request came in the Sovereign's name (*McCorquodale, sup. cit.*; *Lord Advocate, Petr.*, 1909 S.C. 199). This distinction has not been clearly in focus in recent applications.

The Hague Convention on the Taking of Evidence Abroad in Civil or Commercial Matters (concluded on March 18, 1970) deals with the transmission of letters of request. Under Article 2 a Contracting State shall designate a central authority which will undertake to receive letters of request and transmit them to the authority competent to execute them. Letters must be sent to the central authority of the State without being transmitted through any other authority of that State. The United Kingdom has ratified the Convention but not all countries have acceded to or ratified the Convention and these countries (which include some major countries) need not follow the terms of the Convention. On the other hand the 1975 Act applies to any foreign country. This may explain why sometimes the petition to the court under the 1975 Act is presented by the Lord Advocate and, on other occasions, the letter of request is presented to the court without going through the Lord Advocate's office.

The court has a discretion as to whether and in what circumstances it will exercise its powers. The court has refused to order or request evidence from a person who was accused of a criminal offence in France (*Lord Advocate v. Sheriffs*, 1978 S.C. 56).

Procedure

The procedure is regulated by rule 102A. The petition is presented to the Inner House with a request and certificate from the foreign court as productions. The certificate must comply with the terms of rule 102A (2). Problems could arise if there was doubt about the nature of the court or tribunal which made the request. Because the petition is not served on anyone these doubts may arise when an attempt is made to execute the commission (*Morris* v. *Lord Advocate*, 1973 S.L.T.(Notes) 62). The petition will usually name the person from whom evidence is sought, but it has been held competent to seek to examine the unnamed representatives of a limited company (*Lord Advocate, Petr.*, 1925 S.C. 568).

A motion is enrolled to grant the prayer of the petition, counsel is heard, and an order may be granted to examine the witness, usually before a sheriff.

Application for letter of request

The Court of Session will issue a letter of request so that a foreign court or tribunal may obtain evidence. The application is by minute in a process (rule 102).

CHAPTER 16

LIQUIDATION

Introduction

A petition to wind up a company registered under the Companies Acts is presented to the Outer House (rules 217 and 189). The liquidation procedure is regulated by rules 217 to 218M which were added by the Act of Sederunt (Rules of Court Amendment No. 11) (Companies) 1986, S.I. 1986 No. 2298. Reference must also be made to the Insolvency Act 1986, Part IV and to the Insolvency (Scotland) Rules 1986, S.I. 1986 No. 1915.

In the case of a petition which was presented prior to December 29, 1986 the procedure is governed by the former rules which were discussed in the first edition of this book. Because there are many liquidaton processes in existence which are governed by the old rules, some of the relevant procedures in old liquidations are mentioned below (p. 110).

It used to be the case that defects in liquidation procedure could require a *nobile officum* petition to remedy the defects. Now the court has power to cure defects in procedure under section 63 of the Bankruptcy (Scotland) Act 1985 which is applied to other insolvency proceedings by rule 7.32 of the Insolvency (Scotland) Rules 1986. But section 63 does not allow a radical change in the nature of the proceedings (see annotations to the section in *Current Law Statutes*).

The winding-up jurisdiction of the court is governed by sections 120 and 221 of the Insolvency Act 1986. The provisions of the Civil Jurisdiction and Judgments Act 1982 are excluded by the terms of article 1 of the 1968 Convention. Schedule 4 does not apply because of Schedule 5, para. 1 and Schedule 8 does not apply because of Schedule 9, para. 4.

Caution

Those who remember the procedure under earlier legislation will remember the problems which arose because in every liquidation it was necessary for the liquidator to produce a bond of caution before he could obtain a copy of the interlocutor which appointed him. Now every person who acts as a liquidator must be a qualified insolvency practitioner (1986 Act, s. 388). A person is not qualified to act as an insolvency practitioner unless he holds the required authorisation (s. 390 (2)) and unless he has in force caution for the proper performance of his functions (s. 390 (3)). The caution must be for the general penalty sum of £250,000 and meet the requirements of the Insolvency Practitioners Regulations 1986, para. 10 (S.I. 1986 No. 1995). The caution is in two parts, namely, the general penalty sum already referred to and a specific penalty sum in respect of each insolvency in which the practitioner acts. In the case of a company the specific penalty sum is not less than the value of the assets of the company as that value is calculated in accordance with the provisions of Schedule 2, Part II of the Insolvency Practitioners Regulations (subject to a maximum of £5m. See Insolvency Practitioners (Amendment) Regulations 1986, S.I. 1986 No. 2247). A certificate for this specific penalty sum is issued by the insurance company in each case in which the practitioner acts. It is, therefore, possible for the court to order that a copy of this certificate of specific penalty be lodged in the process in the same way, and for the same reason, as a bond of caution was needed under the former legislation. This happened under some of the liquidations which were commenced soon after the new rules came into effect on December 29, 1986. At the time of writing, however, another, and it is suggested better, procedure is being followed. The view is being taken that the purpose of the new caution system is to enable a liquidator to act immediately on appointment. There should not be a delay while he obtains a bond of specific penalty. (A liquidator's appointment takes effect from the date of the interlocutor which appoints him. See rule 4.18 (3) of the Insolvency (Scotland) Rules 1986.) In any event a liquidator cannot be an insolvency practitioner without having in force caution for a general penalty sum. The liquidator is bound to keep the principal copy of any certificate of specific penalty in the sederunt book and to deliver a copy within 14 days to the registrar of companies for registration (the Insolvency Practitioners Regulations, para. 13). No further filing of the certificate should be required by the court.

Procedure

The procedure to be considered is that of a company being wound up by the court. The typical case is taken of a company which is unable to pay its debts. The Court of Session has jurisdiction to wind up any company registered in Scotland (s. 120 (1)). On the grounds for a winding-up petition see section 122 of the Insolvency Act 1986. A petition may be presented by the company, or the directors, or a creditor or a contributory or the Secretary of State (s. 124). The petition may be presented by a receiver (Insolvency Act 1986, s. 55 (2) and Sched. 2, para. 21).

1. The rules have detailed requirements for the content of the petition (rules 217 and 218E). The petition will be checked by the petition department for compliance with these rules. Most petitions automatically will include some details of the company and the petitioner and the circumstances leading to the presentation of the petition. But in addition the following are necessary:

(a) not only the address of the registered office, but any known change within the last six months;

(b) a statement of the nature and objects of the company;

(c) a statement of the nominal and issued capital of the company and indicating what part is called up, paid up or credited as paid;

(d) the amount of the assets of the company so far as known to the petitioner;

(e) the name and address of the proposed interim liquidator *and* a statement that he is qualified to act as an insolvency practitioner in relation to the company *and* a statement that he consents to act (see the Insolvency (Scotland) Rules 1986, rule 4.18 (2));

(f) the name and address of any proposed provisional liquidator *and* a statement that he is qualified to act as an insolvency practitoner in relation to the company;

(g) the grounds for appointment of a provisional liquidator; and

(h) when the appointment of a provisional liquidator is sought whether, to the knowledge of the applicant, there is a receiver for the company or a liquidator appointed for the voluntary winding-up of the company.

2. Service and advertisement of the petition are regulated by rule 218. Where the petitioner is other than the company there will always be service on the company. There may be service on others listed in the rule and it may be necessary to have averments in the petition so that the rule can be applied. Unless there is a special reason for doing so the petition need not be served on the shareholders. Advertisement must be once in the *Edinburgh Gazette* and once in one or more newspapers. In practice the choice of newspapers is usually left to the petitioner to mention in the prayer of the petition and provided that there is at least one Scottish newspaper with a circulation throughout Scotland, there are unlikely to be problems.

3. The petition is lodged with the other parts of a process. There will also be a copy of the petition for the Advocates' Library and an inventory of productions with productions. Productions

may include an extract decree and execution of charge or other evidence of an inability to pay debts such as evidence of service of a three-week notice under section 223. In the case of a company's petition a copy of the memorandum and articles of association will be lodged. Rule 217 (4) requires there to be lodged any document instructing the title of the petitioner and instructing the facts founded on.

4. The date of presentation of the petition is important because if a winding-up order is later made by the court the winding-up is deemed to commence at the time of the presentation of the petition (s. 129 (2)). It is thought that this means the date on which the petition was presented in the petition department and not the date of the first interlocutor. (See also rule 218 (7) (c) and contrast with sequestration procedure at p. 126.) If there has been a previous voluntary winding-up it governs the date of commencement of winding-up (s. 129 (1)). The date of commencement of winding-up is important, for example, in relation to the challenge of a gratuitous alienation or an unfair preference (ss. 242 and 243). The presentation of, or the concurring in, a petition for winding-up (or the submission of a claim in the liquidation) interrupts the running of prescriptive periods as a result of section 9 of the Prescription and Limitation (Scotland) Act 1973 as amended by the Prescription (Scotland) Act 1987. The date of the interlocutor winding-up the company (not the date of the first interlocutor) is the relevant date in considering the effect of winding-up on diligence (s. 185 and, in particular, s. 185 (3)). The speed with which a creditor or a company may present a petition is, in a situation of any complexity, a factor in favour of a court winding-up compared to the delay caused by giving notice of a meeting to consider a voluntary winding-up. If it may be necessary to challenge diligence it also may be wise to proceed with speed to obtain a winding-up order.

5. If a *caveat* has been lodged, no order may be pronounced except after a hearing of parties (rule 218A). In practice a petition department clerk telephones the caveator's solicitors and if possible a date is fixed for hearing parties within 24 hours. The next order will depend on the outcome of the hearing. There may be an order for intimation, service and advertisement or there may not. There may, or may not, be the appointment of a provisional liquidator. The court's powers are extensive (see s. 125). On the difficulty of opposing a first order when a creditor petitions and a receiver opposes see *Foxhall & Gyle (Nurseries) Ltd., Petrs.*, 1978 S.L.T. (Notes) 29.

6. Assuming that no *caveat* has been lodged and that the

appointment of a provisional liquidator is not sought, there will be, without the enrolment of a motion, an order for intimation, service and advertisement. If a provisional liquidator is to be appointed it is necessary to enrol a motion. Usually it is requested that the provisional liquidator be granted the powers contained in section 169 (1) of the Insolvency Act 1986. The motion for his appointment (and for intimation and advertisement and, if appropriate, service) is not intimated to anyone and need not appear in the Rolls of Court. It will go before a judge at the earliest convenient time. Cause must be shown for the appointment of a provisional liquidator (rule 218E (2) and (3); *Levy* v. *Napier*, 1962 S.C. 468; *Teague, Petr.*, 1985 S.L.T. 469). Counsel must appear and argue the position.

7. In the case of a creditor's petition which seeks the appointment of a provisional liquidator the first interlocutor may be in the following form:

> "The Lord Ordinary having heard counsel appoints the petition to be intimated on the Walls and in the Minute Book in common form and to be advertised once in each of the *Edinburgh Gazette* and the *Glasgow Herald* newspapers; Grants Warrant for service of the petiton as craved, together with a copy of this interlocutor, upon the parties named and designed in the Schedule annexed to the Petition; Allows them and all parties claiming an interest to lodge answers thereto, if so advised, within eight days after such intimation, advertisement and service; and meantime until the prayer of the Petition for a winding-up order has been granted or refused, Nominates and Appoints A (design) an insolvency practitioner, duly qualified under the Act, to be provisional liquidator of [the company]; Authorises the provisional liquidator to exercise the powers contained in section 169 (1) of the Insolvency Act 1986, without further intervention by the Court; Appoints the petitioner to send a certified copy of this interlocutor forthwith to the provisional liquidator; Appoints the provisional liquidator to give notice of his appointment forthwith in terms of Rule 4.2 of the Insolvency (Scotland) Rules 1986."

8. The petitioner's solicitor "forthwith" sends a certified copy of the interlocutor to the provisional liquidator. This is required by the interlocutor and by rule 218E (4). The provisional liquidator gives notice of his appointment to the Registrar of Companies, the company and any receiver (the Insolvency (Scotland) Rules 1986, rule 4.2). A provisional liquidator can be appointed at a later stage

following a note in the process (rule 218E (1)). In that event he must advertise his appointment in the *Edinburgh Gazette* and in one or more newspapers (rule 218E (5)).

9. In accordance with the normal terms of the first interlocutor the petitioner's solicitor will arrange for intimation and, if appropriate, service of the petition. There must also be advertisement in the *Gazette* and newspapers. This is a stage at which matters are likely to go wrong. A common problem is the form of advertisement. Rule 218 (7) must be complied with. This requires *inter alia* the date on which the petition was presented (not necessarily the same as the date of the first interlocutor), the date of appointment of a provisional liquidator, and the name and address of the petitioner and, where the petitioner is the company, its registered office. A copy of the first order with designations of the petitioner and solicitor may not be sufficient advertisement.

10. The *induciae* for answers is eight days (rule 218 (8)). An execution copy petition is lodged and also an inventory of productions with the *Gazette* and newspapers. A motion is enrolled to grant the prayer of the petition and for expenses. An interlocutor will be passed in the following form:

> "The Lord Ordinary having considered the petition and proceedings, no answers having been lodged, orders that [the company] be wound up by the Court under the provisions of the Insolvency Act 1986; Nominates and Appoints A (design) an insolvency practitioner, duly qualified under the said Act, to be *interim* liquidator of said company; Finds the expenses of this application to be expenses in the liquidation and remits the account thereof, when lodged, to the Auditor of Court for Taxation; Appoints the clerk of court to send a copy of this order forthwith to said *interim* liquidator; and Appoints the *interim* liquidator to give notice of his appointment in terms of Rule 4.18 of the Insolvency (Scotland) Rules 1986."

11. Normally the provisional liquidator is appointed interim liquidator. If he is not he may lodge a note for his discharge (rule 218E (6); and see s. 174 (5) of the Insolvency Act 1986). In the procedure followed prior to the 1986 Act and which might still be followed the note would seek intimation on the walls and in the minute book and advertisement in the *Gazette* and newspapers; a remit of the business account of the solicitor to the Auditor of Court for taxation; a remit to an accountant to audit the account of the liquidator's intromissions; a remit to the Auditor to suggest a suitable remuneration for the liquidator and to appoint the accountant and the Auditor to confer; authority for the liquidator

to take credit in his accounts for his remuneration and to pay the taxed amounts for the business account; to approve the accounts and to discharge the provisional liquidator. The court may order the provisional liquidator to take payment out of the property of the company (Insolvency Rules, rule 4.6). The amount of the provisional liquidator's remuneration is governed by rule 4.5. This type of application has not yet been presented under the new rules and it remains to be seen what practice the court will adopt. The appointment of the provisional liquidator could terminate because the winding-up petition is dismissed (for the consequences see rules 4.5 and 4.6).

12. The petition department send a copy of the appointment to the interim liquidator because of the terms of the interlocutor and the terms of rule 4.18 (3) of the Insolvency Rules. The interim liquidator must then give notice of his appointment to the registrar of companies (within seven days) and to the creditors and contributories (within 28 days) (rule 4.18 (4)). Instead of notice to the creditors it may be preferable to have advertisement but that needs the authority of the court (or the court may order this advertisement; rule 218D).

13. The interim liquidator summons a meeting of creditors and, if appropriate, contributories for the purpose of choosing a liquidator. The meeting must be called within 28 days of the winding-up order in terms of section 138 (3). The section does not state that the meeting must actually be held within the 28-day period but this appears to be the intention of the scheme produced by the Act. The court can extend the period (s. 138 (3)). The procedure at a meeting is controlled by rules 4.12 and 4.14 and Part 7 of the Insolvency Rules. Twenty-one days' notice of a meeting has to be given (rule 7.3). The meeting or meetings may appoint a liquidator (who can be the interim liquidator) and may appoint a liquidation committee (s. 142). The appointment of the liquidator is effective from the date when his appointment is certified by the chairman of the meeting in terms of rule 4.19 of the Insolvency Rules. The liquidator must within seven days give notice of his appointment to the court and to the Registrar of Companies and within 28 days advertise his appointment in a newspaper (rule 4.19 (4) of the Insolvency Rules). The liquidator should send notice of his appointment to the Deputy Principal Clerk who will cause it to be lodged in the appropriate process (rule 218S). If the meetings do not appoint a liquidator, or appoint different liquidators, application should be made to the court seeking the appropriate remedy under rule 218H and sections 138 (5) and 139 (4).

14. The finding of expenses in favour of the petitioner in the winding-up order should not be forgotten and the procedure for taxation of his account may be started.

The first note

After the appointment of the liquidator the next stage in the court process will be a note. The authors are entering into the unknown at this point because there have been few petitions which have proceeded this far and been governed by the new rules. What follows is a suggested procedure, but there is no guarantee that it will be followed by the court. Experience with other insolvency procedures suggests that variations in practice will arise before the procedure settles down.

1. A note will be lodged which will seek the authority of the court to dispense with the settlement of a list of contributories (s. 148 (2); if a list has to be settled the procedure is detailed below at p. 109. Unlike the note under the previous rules this note does not seek to appoint a committee of inspection because the committee is now appointed by the creditors and contributories (s. 142). Nor is there any reference to the appointment of solicitors. (The terms of section 245 (1) (c) of the Companies Act 1948 and of section 539 (1) (c) of the Companies Act 1985 are not reproduced in Schedule 4 to the Insolvency Act 1986.) The liquidator does not need sanction to appoint a solicitor or any other agent (Sched. 4, para. 12) although he must intimate the employment of a solicitor to the liquidation committee (s. 167 (2) (b)).

The note under the old procedure used to apply for a date to be fixed as the date by which creditors should be ordained to lodge their claims and grounds of debt or be excluded from the benefit of any distribution made before their debts are proved (s. 153; usually a date about six weeks ahead was chosen). This could still be done although the date should take into account that a creditor is entitled to lodge a claim not later than eight weeks before the end of an accounting period in terms of rule 4.15 of the Insolvency (Scotland) Rules 1986. There would need to be advertisement of the note in the *Edinburgh Gazette* and newspapers. The system of distribution of the estate in respect of the accounting periods of 26 weeks which is provided for in section 52 of the Bankruptcy (Scotland) Act 1985 is applied to liquidations as a result of rule 4.68 of the Insolvency (Scotland) Rules 1986. The effect of this appears to make it unnecessary in most cases to apply for a date to be fixed by which creditors must lodge their claims.

2. The note is lodged (with a certified copy and a copy for the

Advocates' Library) and a motion is enrolled "to grant the prayer of note number —— of process." An interlocutor is passed which grants the order sought.

Incidental applications

In the course of the liquidation there may be several incidental applications to the court. Some of these are listed in the rules of court, *e.g.* applications and appeals in relation to a statement of affairs (rule 218F); appeals against adjudications of claims (rule 218G); removal of a liquidator (rule 218J): applications in relation to remuneration of the liquidator (rule 218K); and an application to appoint a special manager (rule 218L). Any application not specifically mentioned is made by note in the process (rule 218M). The note may be intimated, served and, if necessary, advertised as the court shall direct (rule 218Q). On whether a claim for damages should proceed as a separate action or as an appeal against a liquidator's deliverance, see *Knoll Spinning Co. Ltd.* v. *Brown*, 1977 S.C. 291.

Remuneration of liquidator and payment of dividends

Procedure in the liquidation differs according to whether or not there is a liquidation committee. It is the liquidation committee which fixes the remuneration of the liquidator. If there is no liquidation committee the liquidator will have to apply to the court.

The payment of dividends to the creditors and the payment and reimbursement of the liquidator follow, broadly, the scheme laid down for sequestrations by sections 52 and 53 of the Bankruptcy (Scotland) Act 1985. This is the result of rule 4.68 of the Insolvency Rules. The estate is to be distributed in respect of accounting periods. These are periods of 26 weeks. The first period commences with the date of presentation of the petition (rule 4.16 (2) of the Insolvency Rules). This is a curious rule because if there is delay in the early stages of the petition, accounting periods can expire before a liquidator is appointed. Within two weeks after the end of an accounting period the liquidator must submit to the liquidation committee an account of his intromissions, a scheme of division, and a claim for outlays and remuneration. This is the effect of section 53 of the 1985 Act as applied by the Insolvency Rules. The liquidation committee audit the accounts and fix the amount of remuneration and outlays of the liquidator. Therefore, unless there is an appeal against any determination, the court is not involved except that a copy of documents submitted to the liquidation committee must be sent to the court (s. 53 of the 1985 Act; note that rule 4.16 (2) substitutes the court for the Accountant in Bankruptcy). The documents would be sent by the liquidator to the Deputy Principal Clerk (rule 218S). The liquidator can make application to the liquidation committee for interim remuneration (rule 4.32 (2) inserting section 53 (1)A into the Bankruptcy (Scotland) Act 1985).

If there is no liquidation committee the liquidator must make application to the court at the end of every accounting period. This is cumbersome and expensive and is an incentive to have a committee. The application to the court will be by way of note. The contents of the note are a matter for speculation. It will presumably seek remits of accounts and approval of a scheme of division in much the same way as a final note under the old procedure (see p. 110). The audit is supposed to take place within six weeks (s. 53 (3) of the Bankruptcy (Scotland) Act 1985). It is suggested that there need not be intimation or service of the note and it can be dealt with by a series of motions.

Discharge of liquidator and end of liquidation

At the end of the liquidation the liquidator may wish a discharge. The procedure in rule 4.31 of the Insolvency Rules and section 146 of the Insolvency Act 1986 applies. The liquidator calls a final meeting of creditors, puts his report to the meeting and the creditors may resolve that the liquidator is released. Within seven days of the meeting the liquidator gives notice to the registrar of companies and to the court in Form 4.17 (Scot). The notice to the court will be addressed to the Deputy Principal Clerk (rule 218S). As soon as the liquidator has given this notice he vacates office (s. 172 (8) of the Insolvency Act 1986). The Registrar of Companies registers the notice and three months from the registration the company is dissolved (s. 205 (2)).

Unclaimed dividends are lodged in a bank in the name of the Accountant of Court in terms of section 193 of the 1986 Act and the deposit receipts are transmitted to the Accountant. After seven years the sums are paid to the Secretary of State (s. 58 of the Bankruptcy (Scotland) Act 1985).

The liquidator must keep a record in a prescribed form for 10 years from his discharge or the date of expiry of caution (Insolvency Practitioners Regulations 1986, para. 18).

Early dissolution

There is a procedure for early dissolution of the company if after the first meeting of creditors and contributories it appears to the liquidator that the realisable assets of the company are insufficient to cover the expenses of the winding-up. The procedure in section 204 of the Insolvency Act 1986 is followed. Under the procedure prior to the Act the liquidator wrote a letter to the Deputy Principal Clerk of Session explaining the company's affairs and enclosing a final Account of Charge and Discharge. These documents were placed before the liquidation judge in chambers and an interlocutor was passed which dissolved the company and ordered the liquidator to intimate to the Registrar of Companies. No discharge was granted to the liquidator. It is hoped that this procedure will be followed under section 204. The liquidator's letter can be treated as a report to the court which in terms of rule 218S can be sent to the Deputy Principal Clerk. A doubt arises because the terms of section 204 (5) suggest that someone may apply for a deferment of the dissolution of the company. If this were to be treated as needing advertisement of the liquidator's application and the lodging of a note (see rule 218M) there could be the unfortunate consequence that the liquidator would pay for this procedure out of his own pocket.

Settlement of a list of contributories

Under section 148 of the Insolvency Act 1986 as soon as may be after making a winding-up order the court shall settle a list of contributories unless the court dispenses with settlement. The procedure for settlement used to be in rule 211 (*a*) of the rules of court but this was repealed, perhaps by mistake, when new rules 202 to 218B came into operation on December 29, 1986.

In settling a list the court must distinguish between persons who are contributories in their own right and persons who are contributories as being representatives of or liable for the debts of others (s. 148 (3)). A "contributory" is any person liable to contribute to the assets of a company in the event of its being wound up (s. 79). A contributory is usually a shareholder who holds partly-paid shares (and in some cases a person who has ceased to hold the shares within the previous year) or a person who is a member of a company limited by guarantee (see s. 74; there are other examples of contributories). The liability of a contributory is a debt due from him to the company (s. 80) and, therefore, the contributories are an asset of the company in liquidation.

To settle a list of contributories the liquidator prepares a list which should contain a statement of the name and address of, and the number of shares and the extent of the interest to be attributed to, each contributory. The list should distinguish the several classes of contributories. The liquidator applies to the court by note for settlement of the list. The list is appended to the note. The court will order service by post on the persons listed as contributories and allow answers or objections within an *induciae*. There is service of the note, a copy of the interlocutor and either the list, or details from the list which apply to the person being served. After the *induciae* an execution copy note is lodged and a motion enrolled to settle the list of contributories.

Once the list is settled some of the contributories may make payment to the liquidator. If a contributory does not make payment the court has a wide range of powers. The liquidator may apply by note for a call to be made on a contributory (s. 150) or for an order that the contributory is liable to make payment (s. 149). The liquidator may apply to the court for a decree against all contributories liable in payment of calls (s. 161). The court may grant power to arrest a contributory and seize his books, papers and moveable personal property (s. 158).

Old liquidations

Some liquidations which commenced under the Companies Acts 1948 or 1985 will be active for many years to come. It is to be hoped that they have all by now passed the stage of the First Note which was dealt with in the first edition of this book (1st ed., p. 22; see also other incidental applications at pp. 28 to 29). But applications for a Final Note will continue to arise. The procedure is narrated below.

In liquidation proceedings commenced prior to December 29, 1986 (when the Insolvency Act 1986 came into force) the old rules of court 202 to 218B apply (see Act of Sederunt (Rules of Court Amendment No. 11) (Companies) 1986, S.I. 1986 No. 2298, para. 2 (2)).

1. The Final Note narrates the history of the liquidation and seeks:

(a) Intimation on the walls and in the minute book, service on the cautioners, and advertisement in the *Gazette* and newspapers. If the papers in which advertisement is sought are not the same as ordered by the first order in the petition, the change will be queried by the petition department.

(b) A remit of the business account (*i.e.* solicitor's account) to the Auditor of Court for taxation.

(c) A remit to an accountant to audit the accounts of the liquidator's intromissions. The accountant should not be named in the note.

(d) A remit to the Auditor to suggest a suitable remuneration for the liquidator and to appoint the accountant and Auditor to confer. If the liquidator has acted also as provisional liquidator the remits sought under (c) and (d) should deal with this period of office.

(e) Authority to the liquidator to take credit in his accounts for his remuneration and to pay the taxed amounts of the business account.

(f) To approve the liquidator's statement of claims and his adjudications thereon and to authorise him to pay the creditors in proportion to their claims in terms of a scheme of division.

(g) Upon the remuneration and expenses being paid and on payment of the creditors, to approve the final account of the liquidator's intromissions and to discharge him.

(h) To pronounce an order dissolving the company and authorising the liquidator to destroy books, documents and accounts of the company after two years. The period specified should not exceed five years (see s. 341 (2), 1948 Act; s. 640 (2), 1985 Act). Two years has the advantage that it coincides with the statutory period within which the court may declare the dissolution void (s. 651 (1), 1985 Act).

(i) To authorise the liquidator to obtain delivery of his bond of caution. It should be checked whether there is more than one bond or memorandum of agreement restricting caution.

Not all the heads of this note will be dealt with at one time. There will be a series of motions which seek the appropriate heads of the note to be implemented. It is nevertheless convenient to lodge one note rather than a series of notes. One note is cheaper than a series and there is less likelihood of something being overlooked. There will not necessarily be any productions lodged with this note although it will, as with any note, be accompanied by a certified copy note and a copy for the Advocates' Library. No motion will be enrolled at this stage. There will be an order for intimation, service and advertisement and after compliance with this, an inventory of productions will be lodged with *Gazette* and newspapers and also an execution copy note (with certificate of service and walling certificate).

2. A motion will be enrolled, "On behalf of the noter for a remit in terms of heads —— of the note No. —— of Process." These are the three heads of the note which deal with remits to an accountant to be appointed by the court and the Auditor of Court. An interlocutor grants the remits and the business account is lodged in process.

3. The process is uplifted from the petition department and transmitted by the noter's agents for taxation of the business

account and the liquidator's accounts. The reporting accountant will wish to see a copy of the solicitor's account to check if there is duplication (*e.g.* solicitor and liquidator both charging for the same advertisement). The Auditor and the accountant will confer with each other and with the liquidator. When they are available the accountant's report on the liquidator's intromissions, the Auditor's report on the liquidator's remuneration and the taxed business account are lodged in process. From the accountant's report the petition department will be able to check whether rule 213 (*c*) has been complied with (the reference is to the rule in force prior to December 29, 1986). A motion will be enrolled, "On behalf of the noter for approval of the Auditor of Court's report and (the accountant)'s report numbers —— and —— of process and for authority for the noter to take credit in terms thereof; for approval of the Auditor of Court's report on the business account of expenses number —— of process and for authority to pay the taxed amount thereof." An appropriate interlocutor is passed.

4. The liquidator now knows his fee and the amount of the solicitor's account. He should be in a position to know what he can pay creditors. He lodges in process a scheme of division and (if not earlier lodged) a statement of claims and adjudications on claims all signed by him. A motion is enrolled, "On behalf of the noter for approval of the noter's deliverances as set forth in the statement of claims and adjudications number —— of process; for ranking of the creditors in terms thereof; for approval of the scheme of division number —— of process and for authority to pay the creditors in terms of the said scheme of division." An appropriate interlocutor is passed.

5. After payment of the creditors the liquidator lodges an inventory of productions with creditors' receipts and the final account of charge and discharge. The creditors' receipts may include the Accountant of Court's receipt for unclaimed dividends (see s. 344, 1948 Act; s. 643, 1985 Act). A motion will be enrolled to grant the three remaining heads of the note. Before preparing the final interlocutor which discharges the liquidator the petition department will check that everything is in order. The receipts will be examined. To do this properly it is necessary to have the scheme of division, which gives the amount of dividend, and the adjudication on claims, which identifies the creditors and the nature of their ranking. The solicitor's receipt for payment of the business account is expected to be on the account.

6. The final interlocutor approves the deliverances of the liquidator as set out in the final account of charge and discharge. Although it has not always been the practice, the interlocutor

should discharge the liquidator for any period for which he acted as provisional liquidator. The Accountant of Court is authorised to deliver up the bond of caution. The interlocutor dissolves the company and directs the liquidator to report the order to the Registrar of Companies in terms of section 274 (2) of the 1948 Act or section 568 (2) of the 1985 Act. The liquidator is authorised to destroy the books, documents, and accounts of the company and those used in the liquidation after two years.

7. A certified copy of the final interlocutor is needed to enable the liquidator to intimate to the Registrar of Companies. To obtain the bond or bonds of caution and any memoranda which restrict caution, the liquidator's solicitor takes the interlocutor sheet to the Accountant of Court (or while the Accountant's office is outwith the Parliament House complex the petition department will arrange the transmission).

The terms of the *Practice Note* of May 14, 1970 require the process to be transmitted but this is an unnecessary and burdensome requirement especially at the end of a long and complicated liquidation and the terms of the *Practice Note* are not followed. The Accountant delivers up the bonds of caution to the solicitor and endorses a certificate to this effect on the interlocutor sheet which is returned to the petition department and the liquidation procedure is at an end.

CHAPTER 17

MATRIMONIAL HOMES

Introduction

A variety of petitions may be presented under the Matrimonial Homes (Family Protection) (Scotland) Act 1981. The procedure is governed by rule 188D.

The orders which may be made by the court include:

(1) an order to apportion expenditure between spouses (s. 2 (3), 2 (4) (*b*) or 2 (5) (*b*));

(2) an order which allows non-essential repairs or improvements to be carried out (s. 2 (4) (*b*));

(3) an order to regulate rights of occupancy (s. 3);

(4) an exclusion order (s. 4);

(5) an order which dispenses with a spouse's consent to dealing (s. 7);

(6) an order to require payment of a secured loan (s. 8 (1) (*b*));

(7) an order to alter the effect of a decree of adjudication (s. 12);

(8) an order to transfer a tenancy (s. 13);

(9) an interdict to which a power of arrest is attached (s. 15); and

(10) an order granting temporary occupancy rights to a cohabiting partner (s. 18).

Jurisdiction

Rights of property arising out of a matrimonial relationship are excluded from the operation of the 1968 Convention (see Civil Jurisdiction and Judgments Act 1982, Sched. 1. art. 1; A. E. Anton, *Civil Jurisdiction in Scotland* (1984), para. 3.15). This has the effect of excluding those matters from the inter-United Kingdom scheme in the 1982 Act (s. 16 (1)). The result is that in the normal case jurisdiction may be founded using any of the relevant grounds in Schedule 8 to the Act.

Section 3 orders

Under section 3 the court may make a variety of orders which declare and define the occupancy rights of either spouse. A declarator that a spouse has a right to occupy the home may be sought in a petition which then seeks an exclusion order under

114

section 4. A "non-entitled" spouse should not use interdict as a method to exclude an "entitled" spouse from the matrimonial home. The non-entitled spouse should seek an order under section 3 (3) or (4) and under section 4 (s. 1 (3); *Tattersall* v. *Tattersall*, 1983 S.L.T. 506). A petition which was confined to seeking a section 3 order should not try to exclude the non-applicant spouse from the matrimonial home (see s. 3 (5)). The court may also make orders which control the possession of furniture and plenishings (s. 3 (2) and s. 3 (6)). Interim orders can be made but not normally at the time of presentation of the petition because the respondent must be given an opportunity of being heard (s. 3 (4)).

Section 4 orders

Much controversy has arisen over the orders which seek to exclude the other spouse from the matrimonial home. Either spouse may make the application (s. 4 (1)) whether or not that spouse is in occupation at the time of the application (Law Reform (Miscellaneous Provisions) (Scotland) Act 1985, s. 13 (5)). Subject to some exceptions the court must make an exclusion order

> "if it appears to the court that the making of the order is necessary for the protection of the applicant or any child of the family from any conduct or threatened or reasonably apprehended conduct of the non-applicant spouse which is or would be injurious to the physical or mental health of the applicant or child."

This section should be interpreted without the addition of extra words. An interim order does not require apprehension of "serious injury" or "irreparable" damage (*McCafferty* v. *McCafferty*, 1986 S.L.T. 650, which discusses earlier authority to a contrary effect). An exclusion order should not be granted if another remedy, such as interdict, would be sufficient (*Colagiacomo* v. *Colagiacomo*, 1983 S.L.T. 559; *Brown* v. *Brown*, 1985 S.L.T. 376).

Procedure

The situations in which a petition may be presented are so varied that, for the purposes of illustration, it is necessary to assume some facts. The example taken is that of a wife whose husband is frequently under the influence of drink and who when drunk is violent and tries to exclude her from the matrimonial home. He also assaults her and removes furniture from the home.

The home is a flat of which the husband is the tenant. The children are terrified of their father.

1. A petition is lodged with a copy for the Advocates' Library, a process and an inventory of productions with productions. The petition seeks intimation and service and a declarator under section 3 that the wife has occupancy rights (as a result of section 1 (1) (a)), a suspension of the occupancy rights of the husband (s. 4 (1)), a warrant for summary ejection of the husband and interdicts to prevent his return and his removal of furniture (s. 4 (4)). (An exclusion order under s. 4 may be more appropriate than a matrimonial interdict under s. 14 when alcohol is involved: see *Brown* v. *Brown, sup. cit.*) The petition will seek also custody of the children and a transfer of the tenancy (s. 13; and see *McGowan* v. *McGowan*, 1986 S.L.T. 112).

2. The petition department clerk will check if a *caveat* has been lodged. In the absence of a *caveat* a motion will be enrolled by the petitioner for interim orders. At this stage these may be limited to interim custody (see p. 44) and interim interdicts against, say, molestation of the petitioner and abduction of the children. An interim suspension of occupancy rights cannot be made under section 4 (6) without the respondent being heard. Section 3 (4) requires the non-applicant spouse to be heard before an interim order is made which applies to the personal effects of either spouse or of any child of the family or the furniture and plenishings. It may be that an interdict can be obtained by the wife against removal of *her* property (*cf.* s. 24 and s. 25, Family Law (Scotland) Act 1985). In the sheriff court it has been held that an interim interdict can be granted *at common law* to prevent the removal of furniture which is the subject-matter of litigation even when the furniture was the defender's property (*Welsh* v. *Welsh*, 1987 S.L.T. (Sh.Ct.) 30). The motion for interim orders is heard by a Lord Ordinary. If interim interdict is obtained a certified copy of the interlocutor is prepared.

3. The petition is served on the respondent with the first order. This should be personal service if interim interdict has been obtained (see p. 144). Service should also be made on the landlord (see rule 188D (7) (c) and s. 13 (4); and see Form 18D).

4. An execution copy petition is lodged. If no answers are lodged a motion is enrolled to grant the prayer of the petition. This motion will be considered by a judge in chambers. An interlocutor may be pressed in terms of the prayer of the petition.

5. If answers are lodged the petition proceeds as an opposed petition (see p. 12) but motions may be enrolled for interim orders under sections 3 and 4 (see s. 3 (4) and s. 4 (6)). Intimation

of the motion should be made to the other spouse and the landlord (rule 188D (7)). The intimation must be seven days *before* the motion is enrolled (rule 188D (9)). A copy letter and recorded delivery slip must be produced as evidence of intimation. Concealment of material facts by the petitioner may result in the refusal to make an interim order (*Boyle* v. *Boyle*, 1986 S.L.T. 656). For the purposes of proof affidavits may be used (rule 188D (15)).

6. The clerk of court intimates a transfer of tenancy to the landlord (rule 188D (14)).

7. Either party may apply for a variation or recall of an order made under section 3 or 4 (s. 5). The application is made by motion (rule 188D (3)).

Matrimonial interdict

The 1981 Act introduced matrimonial interdicts to which the court must in certain circumstances attach a power of arrest and to which it may attach a power of arrest in other cases (see s. 15 (1)). The procedure is governed by rule 188D. Seven days' intimation before enrolling a motion may be necessary (rule 188D (9)). The applicant must as soon as possible after service of the interdict deliver to a chief constable or chief constables a copy of the application for interdict and of the interlocutor which grants the interdict and a certificate of service of the interdict. Immediately thereafter a certificate of this execution is lodged in process (rule 188D (12)). Recall or variation must be similarly intimated (rule 188D (13)). The power of arrest ceases to have effect upon the termination of the marriage. On termination of the marriage the procedure for notification to the police must be carried out (s. 15 (2); rule 188D (12)).

CHAPTER 18

NOBILE OFFICIUM

Introduction

A petition which invokes the *nobile officium* is an Inner House petition *except* if it is specifically stated by rule 189 to be an Outer House petition (rule 190 (vi)). Therefore a *nobile officium* petition is not always an Inner House petition. Recall of an inhibition, for example, used always to be an Inner House petition under the *nobile officium* (*Greig* (1866) 4 M. 1103) but it is now an Outer House petition in most circumstances, although the Inner House jurisdiction remains (see Chapter 12; Graham Stewart, *Law of Diligence*, p. 571). A petition for the appointment of a judicial factor used to invoke the *nobile officium* of the Inner House but jurisdiction was devolved to the Outer House in 1857 (N. M. L. Walker, *Judicial Factors*, pp. 4 and 125). Rule 189 (iii) specifically gives the Outer House a *nobile officium* jurisdiction in relation to the administration of trusts and the office of trustee.

At various points in this book there is a reference to the *nobile officium*, *e.g.* in a petition for the discharge of a debtor (p. 133) and in petitions relating to arbitration (p. 36). The *cy-près* jurisdiction in trusts (p. 151) is an example of the *nobile officium*. *Nobile officium* petitions are no longer necessary in some instances of defects in sequestration (p. 123 and p. 134) or other insolvency proceedings (p. 99).

In *The Royal Bank of Scotland* v. *Gillies*, 1987 S.L.T. 54, it was stated (at p. 55):

> "The nobile officium has been defined as an extraordinary equitable jurisdiction of the Court of Session inherent in it as a supreme court; it enables it to exercise jurisdiction in certain circumstances which would not be justified except by the necessity of intervening in the interests of justice. Although the court tends to limit the exercise of its jurisdiction under the nobile officium to cases in which the power has already been exercised, it is neither possible nor desirable to define exhaustively or comprehensively all the circumstances in which resort may be had to the nobile officium."

In that case the *nobile officium* was used to reduce a decree. In practice the *nobile officium* is invoked in a wide variety of cases. Some of the recent examples include a petition to resign as trustees when the administration of the trust was moved outside Scotland (an Outer House petition), a petition to seek approval of the constitution of a club, and the appointment of tutors to a mentally handicapped adult (see A. D. Ward, "Revival of Tutors Dative," 1987 S.L.T. (News) 69), a petition for commission and diligence to recover documents necessary for a sheriff court proof where recovery was otherwise prevented by a strike of court staff (*Manson* v. *British Gas Corp.*, 1982 S.L.T. 77), and a petition to keep children in the care of foster parents for a period exceeding that allowed by statute (*Humphries* v. *X and Y*, 1982 S.C. 79). On the other hand a petition was refused when it was held to be the intention of Parliament that there should be no appeal against the decision of a licensing board (*Fife and Kinross Motor Auctions* v. *Perth and Kinross District Licensing Board*, 1981 S.L.T. 106).

Jurisdiction

Nothing in the Scottish rules of jurisdiction in Schedule 8 to the Civil Jurisdiction and Judgments Act 1982 affects the *nobile officium* (s. 22 (3)). In most cases it is obvious that only the Court of Session can have jurisdiction, but the relevance of the normal rules of jurisdiction to the exercise of the *nobile officium* remains to be settled.

One form of petition which occurs with some regularity is a petition for authority to sign a deed. Usually the deed concerns heritable property situated in Scotland and the Court of Session probably has jurisdiction (Civil Jurisdiction and Judgments Act 1982, Sched. 1, art. 16 (1); Sched. 4, art. 16 (1); Sched. 8, para. 4 (1) (*a*)). It is uncertain whether the statutory provisions referred to cover one of the steps necessary to create a right *in rem* over immoveable property, *i.e.* to obtain a signed disposition in implement of a contract. It may be prudent to treat the petition, for the purposes of jurisdiction, as similar to an action to enforce a contract.

Authority to sign a deed

The court may grant authority to the Deputy Principal Clerk to sign a deed where a party persistently refuses to sign a document which he is under an obligation to sign (*Pennell's Tr.*, 1928 S.C. 605; *Lennox and Others, Petrs.*, 1950 S.C. 546) or where to obtain a party's signature is a practical impossibility (*Boag, Petr.*, 1967 S.C. 322). A sheriff now has power to order a sheriff clerk to execute a deed relating to heritage where (a) an action relating to heritable property is before the sheriff or (b) the order is necessary to implement a decree of a sheriff relating to heritable property

(Law Reform (Miscellaneous Provisions) (Scotland) Act 1985, s. 17). In these circumstances it may no longer be competent to invoke the *nobile officium* because that jurisdiction is inappropriate when there is a statutory remedy (*Forth Shipbreaking Co. Ltd.*, 1924 S.C. 489; *Stark's Trs.*, 1932 S.C. 653).

In the simple case the procedure is:

1. A petition is lodged with 10 copies, a process and an inventory of productions with productions. The petition seeks authority for the Deputy Principal Clerk of Session to sign a deed on behalf of a person. Without a motion being enrolled an interlocutor is passed which allows intimation and service.

2. After service and intimation an execution copy petition is lodged in process and a motion is enrolled to grant the prayer of the petition. The motion is starred. After hearing counsel an interlocutor is passed which may state, for example, "ordains the Deputy Principal Clerk to subscribe on behalf of the respondent a disposition of [the subjects] as the said disposition may be adjusted at the sight of the Deputy Principal Clerk of Session together with such other deeds, if any, as may be necessary to give the petitioner a valid title to the subjects."

3. The disposition is prepared with a schedule for details of the witnesses. The petitioner's solicitor arranges for transmission of the process to the Deputy Principal Clerk of Session along with the disposition and the schedule. The Deputy Principal Clerk signs the disposition and his signature is witnessed by two of his staff. The disposition is returned to the solicitor for registration.

CHAPTER 19

RECEIVERS

Introduction

Various applications relating to receivership may arise under the terms of the Insolvency Act 1986, ss. 50 to 71. The court may appoint a receiver (s. 51 (2); s. 52 (2); s. 54). A receiver may be removed by the court (s. 62). The receiver may apply to the court for directions (s. 63). A receiver may apply for authority to dispose of property (s. 61). The receiver may apply for an extension of the period for submission of a report to creditors (s. 67). The receiver may be directed to make good a default in submission of returns (s. 69).

Defects in procedure may be cured without a *nobile officium* petition under the provisions of section 63 of the Bankruptcy (Scotland) Act 1985 as applied by rule 7.32 of the Insolvency (Scotland) Rules 1986. Section 63 does not allow a radical change in the nature of the proceedings (see the annotations to s. 63 in *Current Law Statutes*).

The court which has jurisdiction is the court which may wind up the company (Companies Act 1985, s. 744, applied by Insolvency Act 1986, s. 251). The winding-up jurisdiction of the court is governed by sections 120 and 221 of the 1986 Act. The provisions of the Civil Jurisdiction and Judgments Act 1982 are excluded by the terms of article 1 of the 1968 Convention. Schedule 4 does not apply because of Schedule 5, para. 1 and Schedule 8 does not apply because of Schedule 9, para. 4.

Appointment of receiver

The rules of court have elaborate provisions on a petition to appoint a receiver (rule 214). The procedure is much more expensive than the appointment of a receiver by the floating charge creditor under sections 51 to 53 of the 1986 Act. But the court procedure may be useful if there may be doubts about the validity of a creditor's appointment. The petition is an Outer House petition. The terms of rule 214 are sufficiently comprehensive for it to be thought otiose to repeat them.

Other applications

Other applications are made by petition, or by note in an existing process, with two exceptions which require a motion (although this assumes an existing process (see rule 216)). The procedure by petition is straightforward, with a petition being presented with a copy for the Advocates' Library, a process and an inventory of productions and productions. An interlocutor is passed which allows intimation and service. An execution copy petition is lodged and a motion enrolled to grant the prayer of the petition. If the petition is opposed, answers will be lodged and the petition will proceed as an opposed petition. When the receiver seeks directions there will probably not be a motion to grant the prayer, but a motion to fix a date for a hearing.

Under section 61 a petition may be presented for authority to sell or dispose of property which is subject to a security, encumbrance or diligence. The procedure is similar to other cases, but the interlocutor which is passed by the court may be complicated. The court must consider the case of a fixed security which ranks prior to the floating charge and must make conditions on the application of the free proceeds of the sale (s. 61 (3) and (4)). Where an obstacle to sale is an inhibition the court has authorised the sale but ordered the free proceeds of sale after satisfying the floating charge holder to be consigned in the name of the Accountant of Court to await the further orders of the court. The ranking of an inhibiter is a matter of controversy since the decision in *Armour and Mycroft, Petrs.*, 1983 S.L.T. 453 (see G. L. Gretton, *The Law of Inhibition and Adjudication* (1987), p. 128). A certified copy of the court's interlocutor must be registered within 14 days with the Registrar of Companies (s. 61 (6)).

CHAPTER 20

SEQUESTRATION

Introduction

This chapter explains the procedure in certain petitions relating to sequestration and personal insolvency. The procedure is governed by the Bankruptcy (Scotland) Act 1985, the Act of Sederunt (Rules of Court Amendment No. 1) (Bankruptcy Forms) 1986 (S.I. 1986 No. 514) which, apart from consequential amendments is now rules 201A and B, and the Bankruptcy (Scotland) Regulations 1985 (S.I. 1985 No.1925). There was also an important change in practice with the introduction of fixed diets for the appearance of debtors. The new procedure was published in the Rolls of Court on July 16, 1987 and came into effect on July 20, 1987.

In the case of a petition which was presented prior to April 1, 1986 the procedure was, and remains, regulated by the Bankruptcy (Scotland) Act 1913 (1985 Act, s. 75 (3)). The procedures involved are explained in Chapter 8 of the first edition of this book but their use in the Court of Session will decline. This is not only because there cannot be further sequestrations under the 1913 Act but also because of the retrospective effect of two provisions of the 1985 Act. Section 63 gives the sheriff power to cure defects in procedure (but not to make a radical change in the nature of the proceedings). Section 63 applies to sequestrations under the 1913 Act as a result of s. 75 (5). The result is to remove the necessity for many (but not all) of the *nobile officium* petitions which used to be commonplace. Section 54 introduced a procedure for automatic discharge of the debtor. This applies to sequestrations under the 1913 Act as a result of s. 75 (4). Unless an application is made to prevent the automatic discharge of the debtor, a debtor who was sequestrated under the 1913 Act will be discharged on April 1, 1988 or three years after the date of sequestration, whichever is the later.

In present practice the commonest application in respect of a 1913 Act sequestration is a petition to the *nobile officium* for discharge of a debtor. The procedure for this, and the continuing relevance of the *nobile officium* jurisdiction, are explained later.

Jurisdiction

The grounds of jurisdiction are set out in section 9 of the 1985

Act. Sequestration proceedings are excluded from the jurisdiction rules in the Civil Jurisdiction and Judgments Act 1982 (see Sched. 1, art. 1; Sched. 9, para. 4).

Petitions for sequestration

Assuming the case of a petition by a creditor the procedure will normally result in two interlocutors. The second interocutor will remit to a sheriff.

The Court of Session used to remit the petition to a commissioner who recovered evidence of notour bankruptcy and checked the procedures which had been followed. This does not happen when apparent insolvency under the 1985 Act is a ground for a petition.

While no suggested procedure is ideal, and there can be circumstances which justify a departure from the normal, the following indicates what may happen in petition by a creditor of a living debtor.

1. The petition is lodged with copies for the Advocates' Library and the Accountant of Court, a process, and an inventory of productions. Section 5 (6) of the 1985 Act requires the petitioner to send a copy of the petition to the Accountant in Bankruptcy (who is the Accountant of Court as a result of s. 1 (2)). In practice the petition department transmit the copy lodged with them.

2. Rule 194 obliges a petitioner to produce and lodge per inventory any deeds or writings founded on in the petition so far as within his possession or within his control. Section 11 (1) of the 1985 Act requires a creditor to produce an oath in the prescribed form. Section 11 (5) states that a petitioning creditor must produce with the oath an account or voucher which represents *prima facie* evidence of the debt and such evidence as is available to him to show the apparent insolvency of the debtor. The usual productions are an extract decree, an execution of a charge, and an oath. The prescribed form of oath is Form 2 of the Bankruptcy (Scotland) Regulations 1985. One of the common problems which arises when the petition is presented to the petition department is that the details specified in the productions do not correspond with the petition. There can be discrepancies in the amount of the debt, particularly when there are complications with the calculation of interest and payments to account. The addresses of the parties in the extract decree or the oath may be different from the instance of the petition. For example, a business address might have been used when the debt was constituted by decree, but in the petition a party is designed by reference to a place of residence. Time can be saved if counsel who draft the petition check that any apparent

discrepancies are explained in the petition. An error in an oath can be rectified by the production of another oath (s. 11 (4)).

3. In the case of a creditor's petition the apparent insolvency founded on must have been constituted within four months before the petition was presented (s. 8 (1)). In *Burgh of Millport, Petrs.*, 1974 S.L.T. (Notes) 23 the court held that under the 1913 Act the date of presentation of the petition for the purpose of calculation of the four-month period was the date when the petition was lodged in the petition department and not the date when the petition was first brought before a Lord Ordinary. In *United Dominions Trust Ltd.* v. *Dickson*, 1983 S.L.T. 572 it was decided that the four-month period did not run when a charge which constituted notour bankruptcy was suspended by the court.

4. The requirements for the constitution of apparent insolvency are stated in section 7 of the 1985 Act. There is a duty under section 10 to inform the court if there is knowledge of concurrent proceedings for sequestration, appointment of a judicial factor, winding-up or analagous remedy.

5. The jurisdiction of the court is regulated by section 9. The usual ground of jurisdiction is habitual residence within Scotland in the year preceding the date of presentation of the petition. An established place of business in Scotland may also give rise to jurisdiction. The Court of Session remits to a sheriff court. It is not necessary to aver in the petition that the sheriff court has jurisdiction. It is sufficient that the sheriff court is "appropriate" (s. 15 (1), 1985 Act).

6. The creditor must be a "qualified creditor" which means, broadly, a creditor for a sum of not less than £750 (see s. 5 (4); the sum may be altered by statutory instrument).

7. The presentation of the petition may interrupt prescription of a debt (s. 8 (5)). The date of presentation of the petition is the date at which the amount of a qualified creditor's claim is calculated (s. 5 (5)).

8. The petition should nominate an appointee to the office of interim trustee selected from the official list of interim trustees held by the Accountant of Court. According to a *Practice Note* the petition should also state whether or not the net unsecured assets of the debtor exceed £150,000 (see *Practice Note* of March 27, 1986). At the time of writing there is an inconsistency between the figure of £150,000 and the requirement that an insolvency practitioner has a bond for the sum of £250,000 (Insolvency Practitioners Regulations 1986, para. 10; S.I. 1986 No. 1995 as amended by S.I. 1986 No. 2247 and see p. 100). It is now no longer the practice of the court to insist that a trustee produces evidence

of caution and as a result the requirement that the petition state the amount of assets is redundant. The second part of the *Practice Note* is no longer followed.

9. A sequestration petition may be signed by a solicitor (rule 193). The petition seeks a warrant to cite the debtor to appear before the court in accordance with section 12 (2), an award of sequestration, the appointment of an interim trustee and a remit to a sheriff court. The requirement that the debtor be cited to a fixed diet arises from a change in the practice of the court which was publicised in the rolls of court on July 16, 1987. The new practice came into effect on July 20, 1987. Styles of petition used prior to that date may be unreliable.

10. When the petition is presented the petition department clerk checks whether or not a *caveat* has been lodged. If a *caveat* has been lodged no order may be pronounced except after a hearing of the parties, or with the consent of the caveator. In practice a petition department clerk telephones the caveator's solicitors and, if possible, a hearing is arranged within 24 hours. It may be important for the petitioner to have as little delay as possible because if sequestration is awarded it is deemed to back-date to the date of the first deliverance, *i.e.* the first interlocutor (s. 12 (4); s. 73 (1)). The date of sequestration is of crucial importance because many time limits run from it, including time limits for challenge of a gratuitous alienation and an unfair preference. (A full list of relevant periods is in the annotation to section 12 (4) in W. W. McBryde, *The Bankruptcy (Scotland) Act 1985*, which reprints the annotations to *Current Law Statutes*.)

11. It is not necessary to enrol a motion for a warrant to cite the debtor to appear before the court. There will be an automatic first order because of rule 195. Under that rule the petition will appear in the rolls of court before the first interlocutor is granted. This causes a short delay which may be inconvenient if, for example, a delay of a day could time-bar a statutory challenge of an unfair preference or it is necessary to have an interim trustee appointed as fast as possible. The solicitor should bear in mind also when he wishes the debtor to appear in court (see para. 12). The solicitor who is presenting the petition can request that it is brought forthwith before a Lord Ordinary who may then grant the first interlocutor.

12. With effect from July 20, 1987 a new procedure was introduced to accord with section 12 (2) of the 1985 Act for the citation of debtors in sequestration proceedings at the instance of a creditor or a trustee acting under a trust deed. This new procedure arose out of some observations of Lord Prosser in *Royal Bank of*

Scotland v. *W. G. M. & C. Forbes*, 1987 S.C.L.R. 294. The court no longer asks the debtor to enter appearance in the process. Instead the debtor is cited to attend a fixed diet. The petition department will advise the solicitor who presents the petition that the policy of the court will be to fix a hearing more than 14 days from the date of the first deliverance. Any request for an alteration of the diet must be made within 24 hours of the presentation of the petition so that the first deliverance may give effect to this request. One day a week will be fixed for diets and, at the moment, that day will be a Thursday. The date of the hearing will require to accord with section 12 (2) and, unless advised otherwise by the petitioner's solicitor, the clerk will fix the date for the first Thursday after the expiry of 14 days from the date of the first deliverance.

13. It will be necessary to enrol a motion if an appointment is sought of an interim trustee before the award of sequestration. This is competent under the provisions of section 13 (1). A creditor must show cause. Also it will usually be convenient to request the court to grant the interim trustee the powers specified in section 18 (3) (*a*), *i.e.* powers to carry on the business of the debtor and to borrow money.

14. If an interim trustee's appointment is not sought at the time of presentation of the petition the first interlocutor will be in this form:

"The Lord Ordinary appoints the Petition to be intimated on the Walls and in the Minute Book in common form; Grants warrant to cite [debtor] by serving upon him/her a copy of the Petition and this Interlocutor and Appoints the said [debtor], if so advised, to appear within the Court of Session, 2 Parliament Square, Edinburgh, on the [date] at 10 o'clock forenoon, being a date not less than six nor more than 14 days after the date of citation, to show cause why sequestration should not be awarded; Directs the Clerk of Court *forthwith* to send a certified copy of this interlocutor to the Accountant in Bankruptcy and to the Keeper of the Register of Inhibitions and Adjudications for recording in that Register."

15. If the appointment of an interim trustee is sought at this time the interlocutor may nominate and appoint the interim trustee, give him specified powers and allow him to enter upon the duties of his office upon a certified copy of the interlocutor. No special caution is required by the court from an interim trustee who must have the caution specified in the Insolvency Practitioners Regulations 1986.

16. A petition department clerk sends a certified copy of the interlocutor to the Accountant in Bankruptcy and to the keeper of the Register of Inhibitions and Adjudications forthwith (s. 14 (1)). The keeper is sent also a copy of the first page of the petition so that he may obtain the designation of the parties. This illustrates the need for the correct designation of the parties in the instance of the petition and hints at possible problems if the instance of the petition is later amended. Recording in the register has the effect of an inhibition and of a citation in an adjudication of the debtor's heritable estate (s. 14 (2)). The keeper returns the documents which have been sent to him with a signed certificate. These deeds are put in the process but they have not been lodged by the parties and so cannot be borrowed.

17. The petitioner's solicitor arranges for intimation and service of the petition and lodges an execution copy petition in the process. Many petitions have foundered at this stage because postal service on the debtor has not been successful. With the new system of a fixed diet for appearance of the debtor and the need to comply with the strict provisions of section 12 (2), solicitors are strongly urged to serve by messenger-at-arms. In the early days of the operation of the Bankruptcy (Scotland) Act 1985 debtors appear to have been able to avoid sequestration by the simple expedient of not answering the postman when he called. Now a failure to serve timeously may have the effect of either refusal of the petition or the extra expense of instructing counsel to appear at more than one diet. The attempt to use postal service may result in delay and expense for which the instructing solicitor must bear some responsibility. There can be uncertainty caused by delay in the return of unserved citations by the Post Office. For all these reasons the reasonably careful solicitor will normally serve a sequestration petition by messenger-at-arms.

18. If the debtor wishes to oppose the petition he does not lodge answers but he or she must appear at the diet of hearing. Only if satisfied with a verbal defence might the court make an order for answers to be lodged. It has been observed that:

> "sequestration is a summary process, and it is of the highest importance that dilatory proceedings should not be permitted. The provisions of the statute itself, therefore, require that the court shall act on written *prima facia* evidence, and for the same reason an appeal against an award of sequestration is made incompetent . . . It is the practice to dispose of any objection raised by the debtor at (the stage when sequestration is granted) without proof and on *ex parte*

statements, and this practice has been in use even when objection is taken to the jurisdiction." (*Scottish Milk Marketing Board* v. *Wood*, 1936 S.C. 604 at p. 611 *per* Lord President Normand.)

It may also be said that sequestration is a serious matter and it should not be granted lightly (*Royal Bank of Scotland* v. *W. G. M. & C. Forbes*, 1987 S.C.L.R. 294). It is one thing to treat sequestration as the "end of the road" for a debtor who has been intent on avoidance of his creditors. It is another matter if there are genuine doubts about whether the award of sequestration is competent or whether the debtor has satisfied or given security for the debt (see s. 12 (3) which is peremptory — "shall award sequestration forthwith" — but this may not prevent the court treating a doubt about competency as cause for ordering answers to be lodged).

19. The petitioner's counsel is instructed to attend the diet and move the court to grant the prayer of the petition. No motion is enrolled in the motion sheet for an award of sequestration. If counsel does not appear the petition may be refused. When a petition is refused the clerk of court will require to make intimation to the Accountant in Bankruptcy forthwith and to the Keeper of the Register of Inhibitions and Adjudications after the 14 days for appeal have expired (s. 15 (5)). It is thought that the court should reach a decision on the disposal of the petition. The petition should either be granted or refused. If this is not done, for whatever reason, the debtor is in the awkward position that his or her name appears in the Register of Inhibitions and Adjudications (as a result of s. 14 (1)). The procedure for clearing the register under section 15 (5) applies only where the court makes an order refusing to award sequestration under section 15 (3). If no such order is made (whether as a result of the petitioner's or the respondent's motion) it seems that the debtor would either have to wait three years for the register to be cleared (s. 14 (3) (*a*)) or would have to petition the *nobile officium*. (Note the limited circumstances in which the effect of recording expires under s. 14 (3). Even the consent of the petitioner may not remove the inhibition.)

20. If the petition does not state the name of an interim trustee who is on the official list, the motion to grant the prayer of the petition should suggest a name. While the Bankruptcy (Scotland) Act 1985 was going through Parliament the impression was given that the clerk of court would choose the interim trustee but this is not common practice. An interim trustee must be appointed on

the award of sequestration or as soon as may be thereafter
(s. 13 (1)).

21. Assuming no complications, the Lord Ordinary pronounces
an interlocutor in the following form:

> "The Lord Ordinary having heard counsel for the petitioner,
> no appearance being made by the after designed X and
> evidence having been produced of apparent insolvency of the
> said X, on the Petitioner's motion Sequestrates the estates
> now belonging or which shall hereafter belong to the said X
> (design) before the date of his/her discharge and declares the
> same to belong to his/her creditors for the purposes of the
> Bankruptcy (Scotland) Act 1985; Nominates and appoints Y
> (design) to be interim trustee on the said sequestrated estates
> with the powers and duties prescribed by said Statute and
> allows him to enter on the duties of his office upon a certified
> copy of this interlocutor; Remits to the Sheriff of . . . to
> proceed in the manner mentioned in the Statute; Directs the
> Clerk of Court to send a certified copy of this interlocutor to
> the Accountant in Bankruptcy."

This interlocutor will have appropriate amendments if there has
been a prior appointment of an interim trustee or if the petitioner
seeks powers for the interim trustee under section 18 (3).

22. The petition department send a certfied copy of the
interlocutor to the Accountant. The solicitor for the petitioner
needs at least two certified copies of the interlocutor. One copy is
sent to the interim trustee *as soon as possible*. The interim trustee
works within short time limits. In particular he must call the
statutory meeting of creditors to be held within 28 days after the
date of the award of sequestration and not less than seven days'
notice of the meeting must be given (s. 21). The 28-day period runs
from the date of the interlocutor which actually awards sequestration (unlike many time limits which backdate to the first
interlocutor). It is true that the sheriff can extend the period
during which the meeting may be held (s. 21 (1) and s. 63 (2) (c))
but a court application caused by a solicitor's inaction is an
unhappy start to a sequestration. The second certified copy is
needed to carry out the remit to the sheriff.

23. To remit to the sheriff the solicitor for the petitioner needs
certified copies of the first deliverance and the interlocutor
awarding sequestration. He transmits these to the appropriate
sheriff clerk along with the certified copy petition No. 4 of process.
He should also transmit all the productions.

24. The interim trustee must notify his appointment to the

debtor and call for the debtor's list of assets and liabilities in the prescribed form (s. 19 (1)). The interim trustee publishes notices in the Edinburgh and London *Gazettes* which invite the submission of claims by the creditors (s. 15 (6)). After various procedures the statutory meeting of creditors is held (s. 23). The interim trustee reports the result of that meeting to the sheriff and the sheriff clerk issues the act and warrant of the permanent trustee (s. 25 (2); Sched. 2, para. 2 (2)).

Other procedures

The procedure narrated above has assumed that the debtor is a living person. Where the debtor has died the procedure is similar with minor variations being caused by the statutory provisions (*e.g.* s. 5 (3); s. 8 (3)). The Act makes provision for the death of either a debtor or a creditor during the course of the proceedings (s. 5 (7) and (8)). Various entities may be sequestrated (see s. 6). The jurisdiction rules are different (s. 9). The Bankruptcy (Scotland) Regulations 1985 make provisions for limited partnerships (S.I. 1985 No. 1925, para. 12).

When the petition is by the debtor with the concurrence of a creditor the procedure is simpler. The debtor may sign the petition himself (rule 193). Apparent insolvency is not required (s. 5 (2) (*a*)). The creditor must produce an oath (s. 11 (1)). If the procedure is in order the court must award sequestration "forthwith" (s. 12 (1). Under the procedure of the 1913 Act this had the result that the petition was taken before a Lord Ordinary without any appearance in the motion roll. The current policy of the court favours publication of the motion (the day after enrolling if necessary) but publication will be dispensed with, if requested, on cause shown.

If before sequestration is awarded it becomes apparent that a petitioning or concurring creditor is ineligible another creditor may be sisted in his place (s. 8 (6). The sisting creditor should produce an oath (s. 11 (1)). The procedure for sisting another creditor enables the date of the first deliverance to be preserved as the date of sequestration which may be preferable to commencing new proceedings.

A petition by a trustee under a trust deed or by an executor or a person entitled to be appointed an executor of the estate of a deceased debtor does not require apparent insolvency (s. 5 (2) and (3); s. 8 (3) (*a*)).

Appeals

Where the court makes an order refusing to award sequestration the petitioner or a creditor concurring in the petition may appeal within 14 days (s. 15 (3); see rule 262) and the general rules which relate to reclaiming motions will apply. When an award is refused there is a delay in intimation of the refusal to the Keeper of the Register of Inhibitions and Adjudications but not in intimation to the Accountant in Bankruptcy (see s. 15 (5)). The ability of the debtor to challenge an award of sequestration is limited. He cannot appeal an award. He could seek recall of the award under s. 16 and s. 17 or he could seek reduction.

Transfer of sequestration

Section 15 (2) provides for an application to the Court of Session for transfer of a sequestration to another sheriff court. There are no provisions in the Act or under the rules of court which govern the procedure for this application. If the application is made at the instance of the interim trustee or the permanent trustee there would probably be little need for more than a motion in the original process and it may not be necessary to intimate to creditors or advertise. Should the application be made by the debtor or a creditor intimation would be required at least to the trustee with further intimation and advertisement a possibility.

Recall of sequestration

A sequestration may be recalled under sections 16 and 17. Recall of sequestration is a procedure confined to the Court of Session. The provisions on recall do not remove the jurisdiction of the Court of Session to reduce an award of sequestration (*e.g. Gibson* v. *Munro* (1894) 21 R. 840; *Whitlie* v. *Gibb & Son* (1898) 25 R. 412; *Central Motor Engineering Co.* v. *Galbraith*, 1918 S.C. 755) or remove recourse to the *nobile officium* (*e.g. Anderson* (1866) 4 M. 577; *Macleish's Trs.* (1896) 24 R. 151; *Central Motor Engineering Co.* v. *Gibbs*, 1917 S.C. 490, sequel *sup. cit.*). Both reduction and the use of the *nobile officium* are very exceptional in this context and normally neither would be appropriate if a petition for recall were competent.

Assuming the case of a debtor who wishes to recall the sequestration the procedure would be as follows:

1. A petition with copies for the Advocates' Library and the Accountant in Bankruptcy are lodged with a process, and any necessary productions plus an inventory of productions. The presentation of the petition does not suspend the sequestration proceedings which continue until recall is granted. In some cases the petition must be presented within 10 weeks from the date of award of sequestration (s. 16 (4)). The petition must be served

upon the persons listed in section 16 (2). The boxing of a copy of the petition for the Accountant in Bankruptcy is not treated as sufficient service on the Accountant. The *induciae* will be 14 days (s. 16 (2)).

2. There will be an automatic first interlocutor ordering intimation on the walls and in the minute book, service and advertisement in the *Edinburgh Gazette* in terms of section 16 (3).

3. An execution copy petition is lodged with an inventory of productions and a copy of the *Edinburgh Gazette* containing the advertisement. A motion is enrolled to grant the prayer of the petition.

4. An interlocutor may be pronounced which recalls the award of sequestration. The interlocutor must also make provision for payment of the fees and outlays of the interim and permanent trustees by directing that such payment shall be made out of the debtor's estate or by any person who was a party to the petition for sequestration (s. 17 (3) (*a*)). It is one of the defects of the statutory provisions that they do not make clear who is to fix the fees and outlays. The Accountant in Bankruptcy has agreed that he will do the task, but he is not bound to do so. The court may also make an order for the expenses of the creditor who petitioned for sequestration or who concurred in the petition (s. 17 (3) (*b*)) and an order for the expenses of the petition for recall (s. 17 (7)). The interlocutor will order the clerk of court to send a certified copy of the order to the Keeper of the Register of Inhibitions and Adjudications, the Accountant in Bankruptcy and the permanent trustee (if any) (s. 17 (8)).

5. The effect of the recall is to restore the debtor and any other person affected by the sequestration, so far as practicable, to the position he would have been in if the sequestration had not been awarded (s. 17 (4)) subject to some limited exceptions (s. 17(5)).

Discharge of trustee and of the debtor

A discharge of an interim or permanent trustee is given by the Accountant under the 1985 Act (s. 27 and s. 57). Appeals under those provisions are a sheriff court procedure. A petition for discharge by a trustee appointed under the 1913 Act has few complications so far as court procedure is concerned. The main problems arise in the procedure to be followed prior to presentation of the petition and guidance on this is given in the "Notes by the Accountant of Court for the Guidance of Trustees in Sequestration" which were issued in respect of the 1913 Act and which used to be printed in the *Parliament House Book*.

A petition by a debtor for his discharge will increasingly become uncommon. This is because of the introduction of an automatic discharge for debtors on the expiry of three years from the date of sequestration (s. 54). The permanent trustee or a creditor may apply for deferment of the discharge (s. 54 (3)). Transitional provisions apply this new procedure where a debtor was sequestrated under the 1913 Act (s. 75 (4)). Most debtors will be discharged by April 1, 1988 or at the latest April 1, 1989. There can be an application for deferment of a discharge and so it is possible that an application under the 1913 Act could be presented after April 1, 1989. The procedure will be found in the first edition of this book (p. 63).

At the time of writing petitions for discharge under the *nobile officium* are relatively common and, indeed, are the principal use of the *nobile officium* jurisdiction in sequestrations. These petitions are discussed below.

Nobile officium petitions

At one time *nobile officium* petitions in sequestrations were common. The reasons for them were discussed in "Sequestrations and the Nobile Officium," 1978 S.L.T. (News) 265. Now the sheriff is given power to cure defects in procedure (s. 63) and this provision applies to sequestrations under the 1913 Act (s. 75 (5)). The sheriff cannot, however, produce a radical change in the nature of the sequestration process by recalling the sequestration or discharging the debtor. The *nobile officium* of the Court of Session remains for the exceptional cases. The need for a discharge by the debtor usually arises because he has been sequestrated under the 1913 Act but no creditors have attended the first meeting of creditors or, for some other reason, a trustee has not been appointed. The need for these petitions will diminish as section 75 (4) begins to take effect with its automatic discharge of debtors. The procedure in a petition for discharge under the *nobile officium* follows Inner House procedure and is as follows:

1. Ten prints of the petition are lodged, a process and an inventory of productions with productions such as a copy of the sheriff court initial writ, a certified copy of the interlocutor which awarded sequestration, a copy of the *Edinburgh Gazette* which contained the advertisement of the first meeting of creditors and a statement of assets and liabilities. The petition seeks intimation on the walls and in the minute book and service on creditors. Occasionally it seeks advertisement in the *Edinburgh Gazette*, but provided that all known creditors are identified in the schedule there should be no need for advertisement.

2. Without a motion being enrolled, an interlocutor will be

signed ordering intimation and service. After these have been carried out an execution petition is lodged.

3. A motion is enrolled, "On behalf of the petitioner to grant the prayer of the petition." This will be a starred motion and heard on single bills.

4. After hearing counsel an interlocutor is passed which discharges the petitioner of all debts and obligations contracted by him or for which he was liable at the date of sequestration. It is sometimes also necessary to obtain the authority of the court to dispense with service on creditors who cannot be traced. This interlocutor is occasionally extracted. The petition department issue an abbreviate of the deliverance of discharge for registration in the Register of Inhibitions and Adjudications and also send a certified copy of the interlocutor to the Accountant of Court. He makes an appropriate entry in the register of sequestrations. In doing this the procedure stated in sections 144 and 145 of the 1913 Act is in effect being followed, although these sections apply only to discharges granted in the normal way without recourse to the *nobile officium*.

5. This procedure has assumed an award of sequestration under the 1913 Act. The procedures under the 1985 Act make it less likely that it will be necessary to go to the *nobile officium* for a discharge but a similar procedure would be followed.

CHAPTER 21

SOLICITORS

Introduction

A petition for admission as a solicitor is presented by the Council of the Law Society of Scotland (rule 2). A petition for admission as a notary public is presented by the Clerk to the Admission of Notaries Public (rule 4). This chapter concentrates on those petitions with which the general practitioner may be involved.

Petitions under the Acts relating to solicitors or notaries public are Inner House petitions except in the case of a petition for admission as a solicitor (rule 190 (iv)).

Specific provision is made in the rules for various applications relating to appeals by solicitors (rules 5 to 9). The provisions appear complex, not least because the present rules refer to repealed legislation. Most applications now will be brought in terms of the Solicitors (Scotland) Act 1980.

Rule 5 deals with the refusal by the Council of the Law Society to issue a practising certificate in a section 15 case (s. 16 (2)); withdrawal by the Council of a practising certificate because of failure to comply with the accounts rules (s. 40 (1)); and refusal of the Council to restore a name to the Roll (Sched. 2, para. 2 (3)).

Rule 6 deals with a refusal to issue a practising certificate except in a section 15 case (s. 16 (1)); and the return of documents in a dishonesty case (Sched. 3, para. 5 (4)).

Rule 7 has the procedure for appeal against a decision of the Discipline Tribunal (s. 54).

Rule 8 involves the appointment of a judicial factor (s. 41; and see Chapter 13).

Rule 9 deals with restoration to the Roll when the court struck the solicitor off the Roll (s. 55 (3)).

The rules vary according to whether the time limit for the appeal is 14 days or 21 days or whether there is no time limit. The person on whom service has to be made also varies. But, leaving aside the specialities of the appointment of a judicial factor, the procedure in each case is similar. The petitions are heard by a Division (at the moment the First Division) in chambers and the petitions are not intimated on the walls. The procedure narrated below is that of an appeal by a solicitor against a decision of the Discipline Tribunal but this procedure can be adapted readily to other circumstances such as an application to restore a name to the roll or an appeal by the Law Society (see *Council of the Law Society of Scotland* v. *Docherty*, 1968 S.C. 104).

Appeal against a decision of the Discipline Tribunal

1. Ten prints of the petition are presented with a process and an inventory of productions. The petition must be presented within 21 days of the intimation to the petitioner of the decision appealed against (rule 7 (*b*)). No motion is enrolled and no appearance is required by counsel. The first interlocutor orders intimation in the minute book, orders the Discipline Tribunal to lodge in process within the *induciae* the findings and order appealed against together with all documents lodged by either party and the notes of the evidence (rule 7 (*c*)). Service is made on the Law Society of Scotland and on the Tribunal.

2. Answers will be lodged, the court normally will allow adjustment and eventually the case will go to the Summar Roll. The Summar Roll hearing takes place in private before the First Division who sit in the Conference Room. Otherwise the conduct and conventions followed during the hearing are similar to hearings in open court.

3. The court has power to make such order as it thinks fit (rule 7 (*g*)). It was observed in *MacColl* v. *Council of the Law Society*, 1987 S.L.T. 524 at p. 528):

> "As has been said in a number of previous decisions it would require a very strong case before this court would be inclined to interfere with a competent order made by the tribunal following a finding of professional misconduct for they are the best possible people to weigh the gravity of the professional misconduct in question and to decide what proper orders should be made for the protection of the public interest and the good name of the profession (see for example *Sharp* v. *Council of the Law Society*, 1984 S.L.T. 313 and *Corrigan* v. *Council of the Law Society*, 1st Division, 27th September 1985, unreported."

CHAPTER 22

SUMMARY TRIAL

Introduction

Summary trial procedure was introduced by the Administration of Justice (Scotland) Act 1933, s. 10. It provides a procedure by which parties may, if they agree, submit their dispute to a particular Lord Ordinary. If a party is *incapax* (and therefore incapable of agreement) the court may appoint a *curator ad litem* (*Munro's Trs.* v. *Munro*, 1971 S.C. 280). The dispute must not affect status (s. 10 (8), 1933 Act; rule 231 (*o*)). The decision of the Lord Ordinary is final. The procedure is regulated by rule 231.

Normally the court will have jurisdiction because there is prorogation of the jurisdiction of the court, if the court does not have jurisdiction on other grounds. But in certain circumstances under the Civil Jurisdiction and Judgments Act 1982 some courts have exclusive jurisdiction and in these cases, unless the court with exclusive jurisdiction is the Court of Session, questions may arise as to whether a summary trial is competent (see Sched. 1, arts. 17 and 18; Sched. 4, s. 6; Sched. 8, paras. 5 and 6; A. E. Anton, *Civil Jurisdiction in Scotland* (1984), paras. 7.23, 9.27 and 10.72).

Procedure

The application for a summary trial may start either as a petition to the Outer House (rule 189 (*a*) (xii) or by joint minute in an existing process in terms of Form 40 (rule 231 (*m*)). The petition is signed by the counsel for each of the parties. The prayer of the petition is one of the shortest prayers. It is in the form, "May it therefore please your Lordships to refer the dispute or question set forth herein to the determination of The Honourable Lord X, Lord Ordinary of the Court of Session."

If the parties are agreed on the facts there is a short time limit of six weeks (excluding vacation and recess) within which the case must be heard (rule 231 (*e*)). Because of the considerable difficulties in obtaining a nominated judge within such a short period the parties are advised to contact the Keeper of the Rolls before the presentation of the petition so that a date may be fixed which is convenient for all concerned. The petition will be lodged with the normal papers and a motion enrolled to allow a hearing. The petition is put before the Lord Ordinary and an interlocutor is passed which allows a hearing. If the parties are not agreed on the facts the petition is lodged and a motion will seek a proof. An interlocutor will allow a proof, of consent, and grant diligence for citing witnesses and havers. Proof may be heard in open court or in chambers (rule 231 (*e*); *McGeachy* v. *Standard Life Assurance Co.*, 1972 S.C. 145).

CHAPTER 23

SUSPENSION AND INTERDICT

Introduction

Petitions for suspension, suspension and interdict, and suspension and liberation are regulated by rules 234 to 247. In respect of an application for judicial review the court may make an order for suspension or interdict (rule 260B (4) (*b*) and see Chap. 14).

Suspension is primarily concerned with stopping the use of diligence or reviewing the decree of a court. It formed one of the original reasons for having a bill chamber, the predecessor to the petition department (see p. 1). As a mode of review of an inferior court judgment it has been described as "of very ancient standing" (*Lamb* v. *Thompson* (1901) 4 F. 88 at p. 92 *per* Lord Trayner). The circumstances in which suspension may be used are discussed in D. M. Walker, *Civil Remedies*, Chap. 10. It is not competent for the defender to bring suspension of any decree of divorce pronounced in an undefended action (rule 170A). On the difficulties of challenging sequestration proceedings once apparent insolvency is established see *Wilson* v. *Bank of Scotland*, 1987 S.L.T. 117.

Interdict is an order of the court which restrains a violation of rights. Although rule of court 234 refers to *suspension and interdict* it is often the interdict alone which is important in modern practice (see D. M. Walker, *sup. cit.*, pp. 214, 216). This chapter concentrates on interdict but the procedure on suspension is similar except that two rules specifically deal with suspension of a decree of an inferior court (rules 237 and 242).

Form of application for interdict

An interdict, including an interim interdict, may be granted in the following proceedings:

 (a) In a petition to the Outer House for interdict (rule 236 (*a*);
 (b) Following on a conclusion in a summons (rule 79) and on a counterclaim (rule 84 (*h*));
 (c) In the course of any cause by motion for interim interdict (*Kelso School Board* v. *Hunter* (1874) 2 R. 228 at p. 232 *per* Lord Deas); Administration of Justice (Scotland) Act 1933, s. 6 (7); and see rule 170C (abduction of child)).

It is competent, although unusual, to conclude only for interdict and interim interdict in a summons (*Exchange Telegraph Co.* v. *White*, 1961 S.L.T. 104; and see *Reed Stenhouse (U.K.) Ltd.* v. *Brodie*, 1986 S.L.T. 354).

Jurisdiction

A defender or respondent may be sued in the courts of his domicile or in the courts for the place where it is alleged that the wrong is likely to be committed (Civil Jurisdiction and Judgments Act 1982, Sched. 8, paras. 1 and 2 (10); Sched. 4, art. 5 (3) and art. 24). An interim interdict may be granted although there are other proceedings in progress in another country of the EEC or in the United Kingdom (s. 27 (1) (c)) and although the jurisdiction of the Court of Session is doubtful (s. 24 (2)).

Article 24 of the 1968 Convention has a very wide provision that "application may be made to the courts of a Contracting State for such provisional, including protective, measures as may be available under the law of that State, even if, under this Convention, the courts of another Contracting State have jurisdiction as to the substance of the matter" (see A. E. Anton, *Civil Jurisdiction in Scotland* (1984), paras. 7.43–7.48 and para. 10–43).

Interim interdict

In two recent decisions of the Second Division it has been emphasised that the factors which govern the grant of interim interdict are different from those which apply to perpetual interdict. In an application for interim interdict the question is not so much the absolute relevancy of the case as the seeming cogency of the need for interim interdict (*Deane* v. *Lothian R.C.*, 1986 S.L.T. 22; *Reed Stenhouse (U.K.) Ltd.* v. *Brodie, sup. cit.*). There are always two questions before the court. The first is whether the petitioner has a *prima facie* title and a *prima facie* case. The second question is, where does the balance of convenience lie?

Prima facie case

The petitioner must have a *prima facie* title and interest (*Wilson* v. *Independent Broadcasting Authority*, 1979 S.C. 351). It is not necessary for the court to decide whether objections to the title to sue might be sustained (*Deane* v. *Lothian R.C., sup. cit.*). Because it is a *prima facie* case only which needs to be made out, the absence of specific averments or the unadjusted nature of the pleadings may not be a bar either to the grant of interim interdict (*A & D Bedrooms Ltd.* v. *Michael*, 1984 S.L.T. 297; *Scottish and Universal Newspapers Ltd.* v. *Smith*, 1982 S.L.T. 160) or to the recall of interim interdict (*Group 4 Total Security* v. *Ferrier*, 1985 S.L.T. 287). On the other hand a *prima facie* case may require that some document is lodged to suggest that a contract exists and what its terms are (*Chill Foods (Scotland) Ltd.* v. *Cool Foods Ltd.*, 1977 S.L.T. 38) and issues of constitutional magnitude might need full pleadings and a disposal of preliminary pleas before interdict is granted (*Prince* v. *S. of State for Scotland*, 1985 S.L.T. 74).

Balance of convenience

Many factors affect the balance of convenience. For example the court may consider the difficulty in quantification of the loss to the petitioner if interdict is not granted or the loss to the respondent if interdict is granted (*Scottish Milk Marketing Board* v. *Drybrough & Co. Ltd.*, 1985 S.L.T. 253; *Rentokil Ltd.* v. *Kramer*, 1986 S.L.T. 114; *Phonographic Performance Ltd.* v. *McKenzie*, 1982 S.L.T. 272). It may be desirable to preserve the *status quo* (*Cowie* v. *Strathclyde R.C.*, 1985 S.L.T. 333). The public interest is relevant (*Forth Yacht Marina Ltd.* v. *Forth Bridge Joint Board*, 1984 S.L.T. 177). A delay in applying for interim interdict may suggest that the matter is not urgent and interdict should be refused (*Phonographic Performance Ltd.* v. *McKenzie, sup. cit.*; *William Grant and Sons Ltd.* v. *William Cadenhead Ltd.*, 1985 S.L.T. 291; *Reed Stenhouse (U.K.) Ltd.* v. *Brodie*, 1986 S.L.T. 354; *cf. Highland Distilleries Co. plc.* v. *Speymalt Whisky Distributors Ltd.*, 1985 S.L.T. 85).

Other factors

Interim interdict might be granted or refused on the basis of an undertaking given by counsel (*Forth Yacht Marina Ltd.* v. *Forth Road Bridge Joint Board, sup. cit.*) such as an undertaking by the respondent to keep accounts of trading (*William Grant and Sons Ltd.* v. *William Cadenhead Ltd., sup. cit.*). Interim interdict can be granted but suspended for a period (*Phonographic Performance Ltd.* v. *McKenzie, sup. cit.*).

An appeal against the grant or refusal of interim interdict may succeed only if it can be shown that the court appealed from has not considered all the relevant factors or if the court was wrong in law (*Cowie* v. *Strathclyde R.C.*, 1985 S.L.T. 333; *Deane* v. *Lothian R.C.*, 1986 S.L.T. 22).

An interdict must be in precise terms (D. M. Walker, *op. cit.*, p. 223; *Murdoch* v. *Murdoch*, 1973 S.L.T. (Notes) 13).

Caution and consignation

In modern practice it is not usual to require caution to be found as a condition for the grant or recall of interim interdict. As Lord Maxwell observed in *Wright* v. *Thomson*, 1974 S.L.T. (Notes) 15:

> "While I do not think that in a discretionary matter of this kind fixed rules can be laid down, in my opinion it would not in the normal case, where no question of the pursuer's insolvency is suggested, be reasonable or necessary to make the finding of caution a condition of the grant or the continuance of interim interdict if it did not appear that the defender would have a substantial claim of damages in the event of the interim interdict proving wrongous."

If it is necessary to find caution the provisions of rules 238 and 239 should be examined for the procedure (and see *Tasker* v. *Tasker*, 1952 S.L.T. 152). When a person is unable to grant ordinary caution he may offer to dispone and assign his whole estate and grant juratory caution. The procedure is in rule 240.

Consignation (see p. 16) is distinct from caution, although it is often, wrongly, referred to as caution. Consignation is sometimes required as a condition for recall of interim interdict. It is not necessary in a petition to offer caution or consignation (rule 234).

Petition for interdict

The procedure in a typical case is:

1. The petition is presented with a process and a copy of the petition for the Advocates' Library. The petition should have pleas-in-law (rule 234). The petition may be signed by the petitioner's solicitor or counsel (rules 193 and 235).

2. The petition department clerk will check whether a *caveat* has been lodged (see p. 6). If there is a *caveat* the petition department clerk needs to discover how urgent any application for interim interdict is. A solicitor or an assistant should be in a position to discuss the petition with the clerk. Normally a hearing can be arranged within two days but if the urgency is great the Keeper of the Rolls will place the matter before a Lord Ordinary sooner and inform the solicitors for the petitioner and for the caveator of the time and place of the hearing. The delicate position of the petition department staff should be appreciated. The petitioner's solicitor is in a hurry. The caveator's solicitor insists on time to contact his client and instruct counsel. A Lord Ordinary must be available at the appropriate time and not be kept waiting too long. The rules provide that "the Principal Clerk shall fix a hearing of parties before a Lord Ordinary as soon as is reasonably practicable" (rule 236 (*b*)).

3. If no *caveat* has been lodged and no interim order is sought,

there would be an order for service and intimation (rule 236 (*a*)). In this context that would be unusual. It is normal to seek interim interdict. Where an industrial dispute is involved a special rule applies. The Trade Union and Labour Relations Act 1974, s. 17 (1), provides that:

> "Where an application for an injunction or interdict is made to a court in the absence of the party against whom the injunction or interdict is sought or any representative of his and that party claims, or in the opinion of the court would be likely to claim, that he acted in contemplation or furtherance of a trade dispute, the court shall not grant the injunction or interdict unless satisfied that all steps which in the circumstances were reasonable have been taken with a view to securing that notice of the application and an opportunity of being heard with respect to the application have been given to that party."

(See *Scottish and Universal Newspapers Ltd.* v. *Smith*, 1982 S.L.T. 160; K. D. Ewing, "Interdicts in Labour Law," 1980 S.L.T. (News) 121 and 1981 S.L.T. (News) 99; V. Craig, "The 'Sinking' of the Camilla M.," 1980 S.L.T. (News) 37.)

4. In the normal case if no *caveat* has been lodged and an interim order is sought a motion is enrolled for intimation and service and for interim interdict in terms of the prayer of the petition. The process is transmitted to a Lord Ordinary for the motion to be heard as soon as possible. The clerk is accompanied by the petitioner's counsel, or solicitor, or both counsel and solicitor (rule 236 (*a*)). If the interim interdict is granted the terms of the order will be fully set out in the interlocutor of the court (*cf. Murdoch* v. *Murdoch*, 1973 S.L.T. (Notes) 13), the process will be returned to the petition department and the order minuted in the minute book. The petitioner's solicitor will make up a copy of the interlocutor for certification by the clerk and borrow up the certified copy of the petition for service by the messenger-at-arms. The messenger-at-arms will insist on a *certified* copy of the interlocutor before service is carried out by him.

5. Regardless of whether an interim order is granted or refused the petitioner should be allowed an order for intimation and service (rule 236 (*a*) and see rule 236 (*d*)). An interim order may be sought at a later stage (*National Cash Register Co.* v. *Kinnear*, 1948 S.L.T. (Notes) 83; rule (236) (*a*)).

6. The respondent may appear and enrol a motion for recall of the interim interdict or other interim order. He may, or may not, lodge answers at the same time. It is of benefit to the respondent

to have answers before the court when a motion for recall is heard. The motion is, "On behalf of the respondent to recall the interim interdict granted on (date)." The motion should be intimated (rule 93). When the motion is enrolled the petition department clerk should query whether the motion is going to be opposed and the estimated duration of the hearing. If the reply is to the effect that the hearing will last longer than 30 minutes, the respondent's solicitor will be asked to contact the Keeper of the Rolls so that a special time may be fixed for the hearing. The motion may be granted or refused and an interdict may be partially recalled (*e.g. Steiner* v. *Breslin*, 1979 S.L.T. (Notes) 34).

7. If the petitioner does not appear or lodge answers the petitioner may enrol a motion to grant the prayer of the petition. In this way the petitioner may obtain an award of expenses (rule 246).

8. If answers are lodged to the petition the procedure is different from that of other opposed petitions. It resembles an ordinary action in the General Department. The rules are not specific in their terms but the normal course is for a motion to be enrolled for the cause to be appointed to the adjustment roll. Not later than seven days after the interlocutor appointing the cause to the adjustment roll, the petitioner must lodge two copies of an open record in the petition department and deliver at least six copies to the solicitor for the respondent (rule 247). The cause then appears on the adjustment roll and proceeds as an ordinary action. If the prayer of the petition is refused of consent in respect of a joint minute the decree is *res judicata* between the parties. It is not appropriate to seek decree of *absolvitor* (*Luxmore* v. *Red Deer Commission*, 1979 S.L.T. (Notes) 53).

Breach of interdict

Breach of an interim interdict granted in a pending cause is dealt with by minute in the process (Administration of Justice (Scotland) Act 1933, s. 6 (4)). Other cases of breach of interdict are brought to the court by petition and complaint which, since August 25, 1980, has been an Outer House petition (rules 189 (xxv) and 190 (i)).

A petition and complaint and also a minute need the concurrence of the Lord Advocate as public prosecutor because,

> "no action should be taken by the court for contempt which might prejudice the fairness of a prosecution or put the person alleged to be in breach of interdict in what would in effect be double jeopardy. Although in many cases the facts alleged in complaints of breach of interdict would not, if proved,

constitute a criminal offence, the advantage of a rule of general application to all complaints of breach of interdict is that it absolves the complainer and the court from the responsibility of deciding in doubtful cases whether the Lord Advocate, as public prosecutor, may have a legitimate interest."

(*Gribben* v. *Gribben*, 1976 S.L.T. 266 at p. 269). A docquet which shows the Lord Advocate's concurrence is written on the principal petition or minute.

Complaint by minute

The procedure will be as follows:

1. A minute is lodged in process which has the Lord Advocate's concurrence noted in a docquet. A motion is enrolled to allow the minute to be received and to ordain the respondent to appear at the bar to explain his or her alleged breach of the interim interdict. This motion should be intimated to the respondent or his or her solicitors, if known, at this stage rather than after the interlocutor which ordains the respondent to appear because this may bring the respondent into court to oppose the motion and speed up the procedure. If the respondent appears or is represented at the hearing on the motion and denies the breach an order for answers can be made at that stage. If the respondent admits the breach, he or she will be dealt with. If there is no appearance by, or on behalf of, the respondent, an interlocutor will be passed which states:

> "Appoints the respondent to appear at the Bar of the Court personally at [time] on [date] to answer the alleged breach of interdict contained in the Minute No. — of process; appoints the solicitors to the petitioner to intimate a copy of this order to the respondent forthwith."

Normally the court will order the respondent to appear on a date which is approximately one week after the date of the interlocutor.

2. A certified copy of the interlocutor is obtained and a messenger-at-arms instructed to make personal service. Postal service should not be considered. It is important that the minuter's solicitors obtain the certified copy interlocutor and arrange service as quickly as possible so that the respondent has sufficient time to arrange representation and appearance. Evidence of service is put in the process at the back of the minute.

3. A hearing at the bar will take place. The police will attend on the instructions of the clerk of court. If the respondent does not appear a warrant for his or her arrest will be granted which concludes:

"Grants warrant to Messengers at Arms and other officers of law to apprehend the said ——; Grants warrant to Governors of Her Majesty's prisons to receive and detain the said —— pending his appearance before the court; Appoints execution to proceed upon a certified copy of this interlocutor."

The petitioner's solicitor obtains a certified copy of the interlocutor and arranges with messengers-at-arms for its execution. If the respondent is apprehended on the warrant the messenger-at-arms normally will conduct the respondent to prison and advise the minuter's solicitors. The solicitors should immediately contact the Keeper of the Rolls to arrange for an appearance before a Lord Ordinary as soon as possible.

4. The respondent having appeared before the court, he or she may admit or deny the complaint. An admission is dealt with (by admonition, fine, imprisonment or other order). A denial results in an order to lodge answers to the minute within a short period.

5. After answers have been lodged there may be a motion to allow the minute and answers to be adjusted. The dispute may proceed to a proof and the interlocutor which allows proof will stipulate "an early diet of proof."

6. It may be that the respondent is a corporate body. It is then inappropriate to seek imprisonment or personal appearance of the respondent. The corporation may appear by counsel or office-bearers (despite the normal rule on representation which would require counsel). The procedure is altered as common sense would suggest.

Petition and complaint

The procedure is:

1. A petition is lodged with a process and a copy for the Advocates' Library. The respondent should be correctly designed. A serious error will vitiate the proceedings (*Overseas League* v. *Taylor,* 1951 S.C. 105); an immaterial error will not *(Anderson* v. *Stoddart*, 1923 S.C. 755). The principal petition will show the Lord Advocate's concurrence by a docquet. There will be an order for intimation and service on the respondent.

2. An execution copy petition will be lodged. If no answers are lodged the petitioner will enrol a motion to ordain the respondent to appear at the bar of the court and explain the alleged breach of interdict. The procedure then follows that of a minute (p. 145).

3. If answers are lodged the procedure depends on the nature of the dispute but the cause will proceed as a defended cause in a similar way to the procedure on a minute and answers.

CHAPTER 24

TRUST PETITIONS

Outer House or Inner House?

The rules on whether a trust petition was heard in the Outer House or the Inner House were changed by the Act of Sederunt (Rules of Court Amendment No. 4) (Miscellaneous) 1987 (S.I. 1987 No. 1206).

The Inner House hears petitions under section 1 of the Trusts (Scotland) Act 1961 (variation of trust purposes); petitions under sections 105, 106, 108, or 108A of the Education (Scotland) Act 1980 (rule 190 (ix) and (x)) petitions by trustees for directions (rule 190 (viii)) and petitions for approval of a *cy-près* scheme (rules 189 (*a*) (iii) and 190 (vi)). The Outer House hears other petitions relating to trusts (rule 189 (*a*) (iii)).

The Inner House has exclusive jurisdiction in matters relating to a *cy-près* scheme and if the settlement of a charitable scheme arises in the Outer House (*e.g.* as a result of a multiplepoinding) either of the procedures stated in *Forrest's Trs.* v. *Forrest*, 1960 S.L.T. 88 must be followed (and see *Cumming's Executors* v. *Cumming*, 1967 S.L.T. 68).

Jurisdiction

Jurisdiction in internal matters relating to a trust arises under the Civil Jurisdiction and Judgments Act 1982, Sched. 8, r. 2 (7). The Court of Session has jurisdiction if the trust is domiciled in Scotland. The domicile of a trust is defined by section 45 (3) which states:

> "A trust is domiciled in a part of the United Kingdom if and only if the system of law of that part is the system of law with which the trust has its closest and most real connection."

These Scottish rules of jurisdiction are subject to the priority afforded to the rules of the 1968 Convention (see Article 5 (6) of the Convention and s. 10 (2); A. E. Anton, *Civil Jurisdiction in Scotland* (1984), paras. 5.50 and 10.34).

The Recognition of Trusts Act 1987, when it is in force, will give effect to a Convention on the law applicable to trusts. The Convention specifies the law applicable to a trust and governs the recognition of trusts.

148

Petition for the appointment of a new trustee

A petition for the appointment of a new trustee under section 22 of the Trust (Scotland) Act 1921 or at common law is an Outer House petition. The common law power is discussed in W. A. Wilson and A. G. M. Duncan, *Trust, Trustees and Executors* (1975), pp. 270–272. It is incompetent to combine a section 22 petition with an application for power to sell or to seek power to sell by note in a section 22 process (*Gibson, Petr.*, 1967 S.C. 161). In a simple application the procedure would be:

1. A petition is lodged with a process and a copy of the petition for the Advocates' Library. There will probably be an inventory of productions with documents which relate to the trust. The petition can be presented by "any party having interest in the trust estate" (1921 Act, s. 22).

2. There will be a first order for intimation and service without a motion being enrolled. Service should be on all parties known to have an interest in the trust estate, including any existing trustees who are not petitioners. After the *induciae* have expired an execution copy petition is lodged and a motion enrolled to grant the prayer of the petition and for expenses. This is an unstarred motion. The reported case law shows uncertainty about the competence of appointing a trustee who is not resident in Scotland (Wilson and Duncan, *op. cit.*, pp. 277, 278). The practice is to lodge a bond of prorogation in process before the interlocutor is pronounced which appoints the trustee. A style for this bond is in Chapter 26.

3. An interlocutor is signed which appoints the new trustee or trustees. Where the petition was presented because a sole trustee was insane or incapable of acting, he ceases to be a trustee when the new trustee or trustees are appointed (1921 Act, s. 22). The interlocutor is final and will include a finding for expenses out of the trust estate and a remit to the auditor of court for taxation.

4. The court no longer grants warrant to complete title to heritage. This is unnecessary because of section 1 of the Conveyancing Amendment (Scotland) Act 1938 which provides also that an extract of the decree which appoints the new trustee is a valid link in title for the purposes of deduction of title. For this reason, if no other, it may be necessary to extract the final interlocutor and either the taxing of expenses should be done before final extraction (which ends the process) or the interlocutor sheet should be docqueted by the solicitor to show that the right to expenses is waived.

5. Where the trust estate includes moveable estate for which a written title is required, a warrant for the new trustees to complete

title to the estate must be prayed for in the petition (*Boazman, Petr.*, 1938 S.L.T. 582). The interlocutor normally will not detail the estate but will refer to the petition.

Petition for the removal of a trustee

The court has a common law and a statutory power to remove a trustee. Use of the common law power is uncommon (Wilson and Duncan, *op. cit.*, pp. 293–295). The statutory power is in section 23 of the Trusts (Scotland) Act 1921. The petition is presented in the Outer House. The petition follows similar steps to a petition for the appointment of a trustee. The petition may be presented "by any co-trustee or any beneficiary or other person interested in the trust estate" (1921 Act, s. 23). Wilson and Duncan state that where possible the petitioners should be all the acting trustees, other than the trustee whose removal is sought, and all the beneficiaries (*op. cit.*, p. 295). This proposition is not clearly supported by the authorities cited. The style in the *Encylopaedia of Scottish Legal Styles* has a petition by the other trustees which is served on those interested in the trust estate (Vol. 9, p. 205). It is a matter of circumstances which course is the most convenient.

It was established in *Lees, Petr.* (1893) 1 S.L.T. 42, by Lord Stormonth Darling, after consulting the other judges, that where the ground of removal of the trustee was mental incapacity, the appropriate evidence was medical certificates in the form used in a petition for the appointment of a *curator bonis*. Personal service should be made on the trustee whose removal is sought, unless the medical certificates certify that service on the trustee would be dangerous to his or her health (*Encyclopaedia, sup. cit.*, Vol. 9, p. 205n). It is not the practice of the court to appoint a curator *ad litem* to a trustee who is *incapax*.

Wilson and Duncan state that "wherever possible" personal service should be made on the trustee (*op. cit.*, p. 295). While this is a good general rule it causes problems if the trustee is outside Scotland, a circumstance which may have led to the petition. If he is in England or Northern Ireland the appropriate process server should be instructed to serve the court documents. If the trustee is outside the United Kingdom service may be effected by the methods listed in rule 74B (inserted by the Act of Sederunt (Rules of Court Amendment No. 9) (Jurisdiction and Enforcement) 1986, S.I. 1986 No. 1941 and applied to petitions by rule 195 (*b*)). This may involve service by an *hussier*, other judicial officer or competent official in the country in which the trustee is to be found. But other forms of service are recognised by rule 74B and may be more appropriate. If the residence of the trustee is unknown or service cannot be effected by normal methods there must be edictal service (rules 75 and 195 (*b*)).

Completion of title by the beneficiary of a lapsed trust

The petition is presented under section 24 of the Trust (Scotland) Act 1921. The petition follows the procedure of a petition to appoint a new trustee with certain differences. The petitioner will be a beneficiary or beneficiaries entitled to the property. The petitioner may be the only person entitled to the property. Accordingly there may be no service of the petition, not even on the executors of a deceased trustee. There will be intimation on the walls and in the minute book. After an execution copy petition is lodged a motion is enrolled to grant the prayer of the petition. Usually there is no order for expenses.

Authority to sell

A petition for authority to sell under section 5 of the Trusts (Scotland) Act 1921 is an Outer House petition. A section 5 petition might arise, for example, if an ailing liferentrix, who used to occupy a house, needs the income from the sale proceeds of the house to maintain her. The trust disposition and settlement, however, gives the trustees power to sell only for the purposes of the trust. The trustees need the authority of the court to sell the house.

The petition is presented by the trustees (s. 5). The petition is lodged with a process and a copy of the petition for the Advocates' Library. The productions will include a copy of the trust deed. Service will be on the parties who are interested in the trust estate. If there are two medical certificates which state that service on the liferentrix (or other person) would be harmful to her health, a motion must be enrolled for intimation and service but for dispensation with service on the *incapax*. An execution copy petition is lodged in process. A motion is enrolled: "On behalf of the petitioners to grant the prayer of the petition."

An application for power to sell is sometimes part of a *cy-près* scheme. In that case the whole petition is an Inner House petition and the Inner House have the practice, at the moment, of remitting applications for powers to sell to a reporter. This is not normal Outer House practice.

Cy-près schemes

The complexities of the *cy-près* jurisdiction are discussed in Wilson and Duncan (*op. cit.*, pp. 201–224). Fortunately for present purposes the procedure is simpler than the substantive law. The petition is an Inner House petition. The petitioners will be the trustees who have been appointed to administer the bequest and who have accepted office (*Watt* (1895) 23 R. 33; *Lindsay's Tr.* v. *Lindsay*, 1938 S.C. 44). It is inappropriate in a *cy-près* scheme to decide a dispute as to the title of the trustees (*Barns Graham* v. *City of Glasgow D.C.*, 1978 S.L.T. (Notes) 50). When it is proposed to administer separate trust funds in one scheme it is competent to bring a single petition (*Provost, etc., of Kirkcaldy*, 1973 S.L.T. (Notes) 11; *Provost, etc., of Forfar*, 1975 S.L.T. (Notes) 36).

The procedure in a straightforward case is:

1. Ten prints of the petition are lodged with a process and an inventory of productions and productions. Without enrolling a motion there will be an order for intimation service and advertisement. Advertisement is normally compulsory. Whether the advertisement should be local or national depends on the nature of the scheme. Service must be made on the Lord Advocate (the spirit of section 26 of the Trusts (Scotland) Act 1921 is followed).

2. An execution copy petition is lodged with an inventory of productions and the newspapers which contain the advertisements. Unless the circumstances of the scheme mitigate against a remit to a reporter (*e.g.* if there is a lack of funds) the court will remit to a reporter. A motion is enrolled: "On behalf of the petitioner for a remit to a reporter." This will be a starred motion. When the motion is granted the solicitor for the petitioners obtains a certified copy of the interlocutor, borrows the execution copy petition, duplicate inventory of process and productions and sends the papers to the reporter.

3. The reporter's report is lodged in process. It is treated like a principal writ, and so 10 copies should be lodged. If the report is favourable a motion is enrolled in respect of the report to grant the prayer of the petition and for expenses. This motion may be disposed of in single bills as a starred motion. If the report is unfavourable and it is considered that the matter will require more court time than can be given on single bills the case should be sent to the summar roll for disposal. The motion is, "On behalf of the petitioner to appoint the cause to the summar roll." It is not appropriate to lodge answers to the report (*Scotstown Moor Children's Camp*, 1948 S.C. 630).

4. When the scheme is approved an interlocutor to that effect is granted and a docquet is attached to the approved scheme: "Edinburgh, [date]. The foregoing scheme is signed and authenticated relative to the interlocutor of this date." This docquet is signed by the senior judge of the Division. It is not the practice to

issue certified copies of these interlocutors, differing in this respect from the procedure for a trust variation petition. The final interlocutor in a *cy-près* application is usually extracted.

Petition for variation of trust purposes under section 1 of the Trusts (Scotland) Act 1961

This is an Inner House petition. It is governed by rule 260. Section 1 of the Trusts (Scotland) Act 1961 is concerned with two types of petition. There is power to vary trust purposes under section 1 (1) and power to alter alimentary provisions under section 1 (4). The power to vary trusts applies to a policy under the Married Women's Policies of Assurance (Scotland) Act 1880 (Married Women's Policies of Assurance (Scotland) (Amendment) Act 1980, s. 4).

The procedure in both types of petition under the 1961 Act is similar. For the purposes of the following commentary the procedure in the commoner section 1 (1) petition is used.

The petition may be presented by the trustees or by any of the beneficiaries. "Beneficiary" is defined in section 1 (6). There is a theory that it is better for the beneficiaries to petition because the trustees' duty is to administer the existing trust purposes, but petitions by trustees are common. The petition must be served on all interested parties. In *Phillips*, 1964 S.C. 141 and *Morris, Petr.*, 1985 S.L.T. 252 the court dispensed with service on remote beneficiaries. (Wilson and Duncan, *op. cit.*, p. 158 in its comments on *Phillips* does not express the practice of the court.) If the provision in favour of the beneficiaries is testamentary, and so revocable, no service on them is necessary (*Evetts* v. *Galbraith's Tr.*, 1970 S.C. 211). The court may order service on the truster or settlor or any other person who has contributed or is liable to contribute to the trust estate (rule 260). When service has to be made on children it is sometimes forgotten that under section 2 of the Law Reform (Parent and Child) (Scotland) Act 1986 both parents may be tutors or curators of the child. The mother has parental rights whether or not she is or has been married to the child's father. A child's father has parental rights only if he is married to the child's mother or was married to her at the time of the child's conception or subsequently. If the trust deed has been registered service should be made on the Keeper of the Records or a sheriff clerk (rule 260 (*c*)).

Although service will be on common law and statutory tutors and curators, the court will appoint a curator *ad litem* for each child beneficiary and also for any incapacitated beneficiary. A person under 18 is treated as incapable of assenting to the arrangement (s. 2 as amended by the Age of Majority (Scotland) Act 1969, Sched. 1).

Counsel may act for more than one party, but where there are conflicts of interest it is necessary to have separate counsel for each interest. A similar rule is applied by the court when it appoints curators *ad litem*. The same solicitors may act for all the parties if there are no disputed facts (*Robertson, Petr.*, 1962 S.C. 196 at pp. 203, 204, *per* Lord President Clyde).

Usually the petition proceeds upon a narrative of facts and a draft arrangement which have been agreed by the interested parties. In the normal case the variations proposed are set out in an appendix, on the analogy with a *cy-près* scheme. If the variations are sanctioned by the court, the appendix can be recorded in the register or registers in which the trust deed or deeds are recorded (*Colville, Petr.*, 1962 S.C. 185 at p. 195 *per* Lord President Clyde).

The powers to be given to the trustees must be set out *ad longum* and not by reference to the trust deed (*Nimmo*, 1972 S.L.T. (Notes) 68). The court has refused to extend the trustees' powers beyond those stipulated in the trust deed and permitted by the Trustee Investments Act 1961, although the petitioner could seek to clear up ambiguities in the investment powers (*Inglis, Petr.*, 1965 S.L.T. 326). But the Trustee Investments Act 1961, s. 15, provides: "The enlargement of the investment powers of trustees by this Act shall not lessen any power of a court to confer wider powers of investment on trustees, or affect the extent to which any such power is to be exercised." The First Division, sitting as a court of five judges, has departed from the law laid down in *Inglis* and granted to trustees powers of investment in heritable property (*Henderson, Petr.*, 1981 S.L.T. (Notes) 40).

With the petition there must be produced evidence of the relevant facts such as an up-to-date valuation of the trust fund certified by stockbrokers, an actuary's report and copies of relevant insurance policies (see M. S. R. Bruce, "Variation of Trust Purposes," 1967 S.L.T. (News) 193). A statement of tax payable on certain contingencies, certified by solicitors, used to be lodged as a production to satisfy the court that there was a material advantage to be gained. It is no longer common practice to lodge a statement of tax.

The procedure is as follows:

1. Ten prints of the petition are lodged with a process, an inventory of productions and productions. A motion is enrolled: "On behalf of the petitioner for an order for intimation and service

and for the appointment of a curator *ad litem* to —, designed in the petition." The motion will be starred. If no curator *ad litem* is needed there is no necessity for a motion and there will be the usual first order for intimation and service.

2. After the interlocutor is signed, intimation and service are carried out. The petition must be served on the Keeper of the Records of Scotland, or on the sheriff clerk of the sheriffdom in which the trust deed is registered (rule 260). The Keeper of the Records should be served at West Register House. He should not be served at Meadowbank House. On receipt of the service copy of the petition the Scottish Record Office make a note on the original deed and in their volumes of copy deeds. The note states that an action is pending under the Trusts (Scotland) Act 1961. The petitioners' solicitor will inform the curators *ad litem* of the details of the process. The curators are appointed from lists kept by the clerks to the Divisions and it is not necessary on each occasion for a member of the Bar who is on the lists to take the oath *de fideli administratione*.

3. An execution copy petition is lodged. Minutes of consent must be lodged on behalf of all the beneficiaries who are capable of consenting. If any of these beneficiaries refuses consent, the trust cannot be varied. Minutes must be lodged on behalf of all the curators *ad litem* and a minute states the view adopted by the curator *ad litem*. Minutes should also be lodged by other parties who are interested in the trust and on whom service has been made. In *Findlay's, Petrs.*, 1962 S.C. 210 it was observed that all parties concerned, even though not opposing the petition, should lodge minutes and appear or be represented at the hearing because their interests might be affected if the arrangement had to be amended. In current practice this is not applied to all remote beneficiaries.

4. A motion is enrolled: "On behalf of the petitioner to appoint the cause to the summar roll." The summar roll cases are heard by the First Division and the last two days of each term are set aside for their disposal. Prior to the hearing four copies of the productions must be lodged for the judges, although in many cases it is the practice for the petitioner's solicitors to prepare and produce four copies of an appendix which contains all the relevant documents. If the hearing is successful an interlocutor will be granted which approves the arrangement. The arrangement may have needed amendment, in which case the minutes will be altered to show consent to the amendment. A docquet will be attached to the approved arrangement in the form: "Edinburgh [date]. The foregoing arrangement is signed and authenticated relative to the

interlocutor of this date." This is signed by the senior judge of the Division. The interlocutor will be in a form similar to this:

> "The Lords, having heard counsel for the parties and considered the Petition together with the minutes of consent numbers — and — of process, approve the Arrangement set forth in the appendix to the petition on behalf of [names and reference to the trust deed]; appoint a copy of this interlocutor together with a copy of said arrangement certified by the solicitors for the Petitioners to be registered in the Books of Council and Session, and decern."

5. So that the terms of the interlocutor may be complied with, the clerk in the petition department makes up a certified copy of the interlocutor. The solicitor makes up and certifies a copy of the arrangement. This is married to the certified copy interlocutor by the solicitor who takes the two documents to the Inland Revenue stamp duty office. After stamp duty is paid, the documents are stitched up and transmitted to the Books of Council and Session or, if appropriate, the sheriff court books. A letter which confirms the variation is sent by the petition department clerk to the relevant keeper of the records. The solicitor will obtain an extract of the documents. In the case of registration in the Books of Council and Session, Meadowbank House will at some time send the original deeds to West Register House and an entry on the original trust deed or deeds is made.

6. The arrangement may require an insurance policy to be effected within a time limit. The interlocutor does not refer to this but the approved arrangement will have a clause which states that best endeavours will be used to effect insurance within 28 days or 30 days. The court has refused to alter or extend the period when, by oversight, the petitioner did not obtain a policy within the stipulated time (*Hutchison, Petr.*, 1965 S.C. 240).

7. If by mistake all the interested parties have not been called, the court will not alter its final interlocutor. This was decided in *Bailey, Petrs.*, 1969 S.L.T. (Notes) 70. There may be some sympathy for the counsel and solicitors in that case who were unaware that a child had been born to a beneficiary after presentation of the petition. There is a moral in this for the petitioners' solicitors.

Petition by trustees for directions
Under section 17 (vi) of the Administration of Justice (Scotland) Act 1933 power was given to the Court of Session to provide by Act of Sederunt for trustees under a trust deed to obtain the

direction of the court on questions relating to the investment, distribution, management or administration of the trust estate, or the exercise of any power vested in, or the performance of any duty imposed on, the trustees. The present provisions are in rules 232 and 233. The petitioners must be trustees under a trust deed as defined by the Trusts (Scotland) Act 1921 (rule 232; *Lowlands Territorial Assoc.* v. *Lord Advocate*, 1971 S.C. 125).

Shortly after the 1933 Act there was a series of reported cases which showed a disinclination on the part of the court to favour a petition for directions, particularly if another course, such as a special case, was more appropriate (*Andrew's Trs.* v. *Maddeford*, 1935 S.C. 857; *Peel's Tr.* v. *Drummond*, 1936 S.C. 786; *Henderson's Tr.* v. *Henderson*, 1938 S.C. 461; *Grant's Tr.* v. *Hunter*, 1938 S.C. 501). The difficulty appeared to be the decision of some complex question in a petition with a relatively informal procedure and an *ex parte* application. This attitude probably explains why the number of petitions disposed of by the court decreased at that time. The number of petitions remains at a low level.

The petition is presented to the Inner House (rule 190 (vii)). In a straightforward case the procedure is as follows:

1. Ten copies of the petition are lodged with a process, inventory of productions and productions. If the appointment of a curator *ad litem* is needed, a motion is enrolled: "On behalf of the petitioners for an order for intimation and service and for the appointment of a curator *ad litem* to ——, designed in the petition." The motion will be starred. If no curator is needed there will be an order for intimation and service without a motion being enrolled.

2. After the interlocutor is signed, intimation and service is carried out and the curators *ad litem* informed of the details of the process. A curator will lodge a minute in process which states his attitude. An execution copy petition is lodged. Any party who wishes to support or oppose the petition should lodge a minute (rule 233 (*b*)).

3. A motion is enrolled: "On behalf of the petitioners to appoint the cause to the summar roll" (rule 233 (*c*)). Prior to the hearing four copies of productions should be lodged for the judges. The court may remit to a judge of the Inner House to hear a proof, or remit to a reporter or require affidavits (rule 233 (*c*)).

CHAPTER 25

MISCELLANEOUS PETITIONS

Introduction

This chapter lists uncommon petitions for some of which there are special rules of court.

Blood samples

From time to time there have been attempts to obtain a court order to allow blood samples to be taken from a person. The usual reason is to provide evidence of who may be the parent of a child. Authority to take blood samples has been refused (*Whitehall* v. *Whitehall*, 1958 S.C. 252) and granted (*Docherty* v. *McGlynn*, 1983 S.C. 202; sequel, 1985 S.L.T. 237). In recent years several petitions have been presented to the *nobile officium* of the Inner House (*Devlin*, P50/1/84; *McManus*, P51/1/84; *Griffen*, P41/1/86). Section 6 of the Law Reform (Parent and Child) (Scotland) Act 1986 provides for taking a blood sample to obtain evidence which relates to parentage. Where a blood sample is sought from a person who is incapable of giving consent the court may, in certain circumstances, give consent. The application to the court is by motion in a depending process or if no cause is in progress by petition to the Outer House (rule 260F).

Conveyancing (Scotland) Act 1874

A petition under the Act is an Outer House petition (rule 189 (*a*) (viii). The usual use of the Act is a petition under section 39 to cure informalities in the execution of a deed.

Defamation Act 1952

Section 4 (4) provides for the fulfilment of an offer of amends in a case of unintentional defamation. The procedure is governed by rule 188A.

Education (Scotland) Acts

Rule 190(x) provides that petitions under sections 105, 106, 108 or 108A of the Education (Scotland) Act 1980 are Inner House petitions. This new rule was inserted by the Act of Sederunt (Rules of Court Amendment No. 4) (Miscellaneous) 1987; S.I. 1987 No. 1206.

Election petitions

A petition may be presented under the Representation of the People Act 1983 as amended by the Representation of the People Act 1985. There are detailed provisions for the procedure in rules 297 to 331.

Entail Acts

New entails have been impossible since the Entail (Scotland) Act 1914, but occasionally a petition is presented in relation to an existing entail. It is an Outer House petition (rule 189 (a) (vi) and the procedure is described in J. A. Maclaren, *Bill Chamber Practice* (1915), Chap. VII.

Guardianship Act 1973

Rule 260A makes provision for applications under the Guardianship Act 1973, but section 10 of the Act is repealed by the Law Reform (Parent and Child) (Scotland) Act 1986.

House of Lords petitions

The procedure for applying a judgment of the House of Lords on appeal from the Court of Session is by way of petition to the Inner House of the Court of Session. The proper way is to proceed by petition and not by motion alone (*Millar* v. *Glasgow Corp.*, 1947 S.L.T. (Notes) 22). In carrying out the decree of the House of Lords the Court of Session acts in a purely administrative capacity. The House of Lords decree must be repeated according to its terms without any alteration such as a variation of the award of expenses (*Maclachlan's Trs.* v. *Yuill's Trs.*, 1939 S.C. 500; *Grant* v. *Sun Shipping Co.*, 1949 S.C. 19). When the House of Lords simply affirms a judgment of the Court of Session, a petition to apply the judgment of the House of Lords is incompetent (*Ricketts* (1861) 23 D. 1014; *Morris* (1866) 5 M. 112; *Peters* v. *Mags. of Greenock* (1893) 20 R. 924).

The petition is an Inner House application and a petition with 10 copies should be lodged. The petition repeats the terms of the interlocutors which were appealed against and the terms of the judgment of the House of Lords and prays for the Court of Session to apply the judgment of the House of Lords. Normally there would not be a first order for intimation and service. The petition is intimated to the other parties and a certificate of intimation written on the principal petition (see J. A. Maclaren, *Court of Session Practice*, p. 927). A motion would be enrolled to grant the prayer of the petition and this motion would be intimated to the other parties along with the petition. The motion would be heard on single bills.

Lands Clauses Consolidation (Scotland) Act 1845

A petition under the 1845 Act is an Outer House petition (rule 189 (*a*) (xi)).

Local Government (Scotland) Act 1973

A petition under section 75 (2) of the 1973 Act is an Outer House petition as a result of rule 189 (*a*) (xxviii) which was added by the Act of Sederunt (Rules of Court Amendment No. 4) (Miscellaneous) 1987 (S.I. 1987 No. 1206).

Merchant Shipping (Liner Conferences) Act 1982

A petition under the Act is governed by rules 249B and 249C. A "liner conference" is the unlikely name for an agreement between shipping lines which fixes freight charges for international carriage. This form of cartel is subject to international convention and the court could be involved in the recognition and enforcement of recommendations made by conciliators.

Mines (Working Facilities and Supports) Act 1966

Applications under the 1966 Act are regulated by rule 259.

Mortgaging of Aircraft Order 1972

A petition under the Mortgaging of Aircraft Order 1972 (S.I. 1972 No. 1268 as amended by S.I. 1981 No. 611) is now an Outer House petition (rule 189(*a*)(xxix) which was added by the Act of Sederunt (Rules of Court Amendment No. 4) (Miscellaneous) 1987; S.I. 1987 No. 1206). The 1972 Order laid down a scheme for the registration of a mortgage over an aircraft and its spare parts. A register of aircraft mortgages is kept by the Civil Aviation Authority. The Court of Session has power to rectify errors in the register (para. 10). When it is sought to enforce a mortgage the court may be asked to grant a warrant for possession of the aircraft. Schedule 2, Part 1, para. 11(1) has rules on whom the application must be served. The court may also be asked to dispense with the consent of other mortgagees to a sale (Sched. 2, Part 1, para. 9).

Proceedings for the rectification of the register of aircraft mortgages are excluded from the inter-United Kingdom scheme and the Scottish scheme of jurisdiction rules in the Civil Jurisdiction and Judgments Act 1982 (Sched. 5, para. 8; Sched. 9, para. 8).

Patents

An application which relates to patents or registered designs may be an Outer House petition (rule 189 (a) (xvii)) to which rules 250 to 257H apply. The petition is heard by the patent judge.

Petitions and complaints

A petition and complaint is an Inner House petition other than in cases of breach of interdict (rule 190 (i)). The use of this petition in the case of breach of interdict has been explained already (p. 147). A petition and complaint may be used also to remove an inferior judge, clerk of court, judicial factor and others connected with the administration of justice (J. A. Maclaren, *Court of Session Practice*, p. 914; see also rule 190(iii)).

Possession or specific performance

A petition for possession or specific performance is an Inner House petition (rule 190(ii)). The use of this form of petition for possessory remedies probably was more common in the past (see J. A. Maclaren, *Court of Session Practice*, p. 639). Many possessory problems can be solved by interdict or an action for specific performance. It is thought that most claims for specific performance or actions *ad factum praestandum* proceed by way of summons. But it has been known for a petition to seek implement of a lease and to request an interim order (see Administration of Justice (Scotland) Act 1933, s. 6 (7)). In this way it is possible to compel performance of a contract with some speed. But the full extent of the specific performance jurisdiction has yet to be decided and if there were difficult and disputed issues procedure by petition might be inappropriate (see p. 2).

Railway and Canal Commission

Applications which relate to the Railway and Canal Commission may be governed by rules 258 or 259.

Rectification of a deed

An application for rectification of a deed under section 8 of the Law Reform (Miscellaneous Provisions) (Scotland) Act 1985 may be made by petition presented to the Outer House, or by summons where ancillary to other conclusions (rule 189 (c)).

Special Roads Act 1949

An application under the 1949 Act is an Outer House petition in terms of rule 189 (a) (xix), but the Act was repealed by the Roads (Scotland) Act 1984.

Telegraph Acts

Rule 258 applies to references under two Telegraph Acts which were repealed by the Telecommunications Act 1984.

Vexatious litigant

Under the Vexatious Actions (Scotland) Act 1898 the Lord Advocate may apply to the Inner House for an order that a person is a vexatious litigant. The effect of the order is that the person requires the leave of a Lord Ordinary to institute court proceedings. Examples include *Lord Advocate* v. *Gracie*, 1951 S.C. 256; *Lord Advocate* v. *Rizza*, 1962 S.L.T. (Notes) 8; *Lord Advocate* v. *Henderson*, 1983 S.L.T. 518 and *Lord Advocate* v. *Cooney*, 1984 S.L.T. 434. The decision of the Lord Ordinary is final (s. 1A of the 1898 Act, added by Law Reform (Miscellaneous Provisions) (Scotland) Act 1980, s. 19).

CHAPTER 26

STYLES

Introduction

Some styles of motion will be found at the appropriate place in the text. The styles here are those which are not readily available elsewhere.

Walling certificate

Edinburgh —— [date], I, clerk to —— hereby certify that the foregoing petition/note and deliverance have been intimated in the minute book and that the said petition/note has been walled and served upon the parties named in the schedule conform to the foregoing execution (or holograph acceptance) of service (and advertised conform to advertisement produced herewith) that the *induciae* have expired (and that no answers have been lodged).

(Signed)

Bond of prorogation in a curatory

I, A [design], CONSIDERING THAT a petition has been or is about to be presented in the Court of Session for the appointment of me as *curator bonis* to B, formerly residing at —— and presently a patient at —— AND FURTHER CONSIDERING THAT I reside furth of Scotland and that it is necessary that in the event of my being appointed *curator bonis* to the said B, that I should formally prorogate the jurisdiction of the Court of Session, THEREFORE I DO HEREBY bind myself if appointed as aforesaid to lodge accounts annually with the Accountant of Court and otherwise to conduct the affairs of the curatory estate in all respects in conformity with the law and practice of Scotland, to appear before the Lords of Council and Session in Scotland when required to answer for my conduct as *curator bonis* aforesaid or in connection with any matter arising out of the curatory, to submit myself to and prorogate the jurisdiction of the Court of Session for these purposes and I assign —— as an address in Scotland where I may be cited.

(Tested, holograph, or
adopted as holograph.)

(The address which is assigned for citation may be the address of the Edinburgh solicitors who act in the petition. There is no time limit for the lodging of this bond although a certified copy of the interlocutor which appoints the curator will not be issued until this bond and the bond of caution are lodged. It follows that the bond could be signed after the appointing interlocutor. In that case the bond may start:

> I, A [design], CONSIDERING THAT on [date] I was appointed *curator bonis* to B, formerly residing at —— and presently a patient at —— in terms of an interlocutor of that date pronounced by Lord —— in a petition in the Court of Session at my instance (or as appropriate) AND FURTHER CONSIDERING THAT [continue as in previous style making the obvious alterations to take account of the fact of appointment].

Bond of prorogation in petition for appointment of new trustees

> I, A [design], CONSIDERING THAT a petition has been or is about to be presented in the Court of Session at the instance of [design petitioner] for the appointment of new trustees on the trust estate constituted by the trust disposition and settlement of —— dated —— and registered in the Books of Council and Session on —— AND FURTHER CONSIDERING THAT I reside furth of Scotland and that it is necessary in the event of my being appointed as trustee under the said trust disposition and settlement, that I should formally prorogate the jurisdiction of the Court of Session, THEREFORE I DO HEREBY bind myself if appointed as aforesaid to submit to and prorogate the jurisdiction of the Court of Session in all matters affecting the trust and I assign —— as an address in Scotland where I may be cited.

(Tested, holograph, or adopted as holograph.)

Certificate of compliance by judicial factor with rule 201 (h)

> I, A [design], judicial factor on the estate of —— hereby certify that I have this day forwarded by post to each of the persons mentioned in the annexed list, being all the known creditors or persons interested in the estate, a notice intimating that the State of Funds of the said estate and Scheme of Division thereof and report thereon, have been lodged in court, and stating the amount for which each creditor has been ranked, and the amount of the proposed dividend which will be payable to those creditors who have lodged claims against the estate and who are entitled to

receive the said dividend on their claim, and in the case of persons interested who have not lodged claims against the estate, or whose claims have been rejected, that no dividend is allotted to them in the Scheme of Division.

(Signed)

1. Attach copy notice of intimation and any other documents sent to creditors.

2. Attach list of creditors.

INDEX